Six Days

The Dean
Chester Cathedral

7th May 2000

Dear Sir

I am writing to confirm my interest in the design of the new
Millennium window for the Refectory West Window of Chester
Cathedral.

I am very excited about the project and have been drawing and
developing my ideas. I hope to visit the cathedral with my
partner and personal assistant on Tuesday 9th May.

I have a slight concern about the time scale of the project. It is
a very large window and hopefully it will last till the next
millennium. From November to May seems a short time to
make a window worthy of the building.

I shall be sending my initial ideas and designs soon.

Yours faithfully

Rosalind Grimshaw

"Stained glass looks quite simple. The material is light itself. For a cathedral or a synagogue the phenomenon is the same: something mystical that passes through the window. And yet I was very afraid, as afraid as when keeping a first tryst.

Theory, technique - what's that? The material. Light. There's Creation. In painting, the canvas and paints are the material. There remains the talent that the artist brings, the spiritual. Precaution is two against one - the combat is unequal! Corot, Cézanne, Bonnard and Monet are victorious. But the others? In ceramics or stained glass it is still worse! What do I bring to the material? To the Lord's earth, to the Lord's fire, to the leaf, the bark, the light? Perhaps the memory of my father or my mother or my childhood and of my people during perhaps 1000 years - perhaps my heart. One must be humble before the material - submissive. The material is natural and everything that is natural is religious. It is when he is in a minority before Nature that the artist has the most luck with it - if he is submissive.

I have all the advantage on my side: the light is that of heaven - that is what gives the colour. The fire that baked the glass and lead also comes from heaven even though it has been supplied by gas and electricity. I have the material and I wonder — is what I bring good or not? If what I have done is good beside the material then I have won because God is behind me. When I engraved the Bible I went to Israel and found both light and earth, the material. When one is 20 years old one doesn't think of the material. You have to have passed through suffering or become old. Sometimes they say to me "But Chagall, you are not material" and I reply "I must stop being material in order to listen to the material. Every colour ought to encourage prayer. As for me I can't pray. I just work."

Marc Chagall

Six Days

The story of the making
of the Chester Cathedral
Creation Window

Created by Rosalind Grimshaw

Written by Painton Cowen

Alastair Sawday Publishing

Rosalind's Dedication

To Henry Luis Ivor Neuburger
06.10.43 – 09.12.98

Who tried to kill me at least three times
Who did everything before me and usually
better, compelling me to form the Y.S.C*
Who taught me to understand
simultaneous equations
Who knew everything, including all the
words and tunes of every song I knew;
even "A goldfish swam in a big glass bowl"
And the location of all Somerset
perpendicular towers, (always had a local
copy of Pevsner)
He thought the third London airport should
be in Calais,
And everyone says how proud he would
have been of his little sister.

2 February 2003

* Younger Siblings Club

Written and researched by Painton Cowen
Published by Alastair Sawday Publishing
Editor: Alastair Sawday
Administration Assistant: Danielle Williams
Design: Springboard Design Partnership, Bristol
Marketing: Jayne Warren PR
Printing: G. Canale & C. S.p.A.

Photographs of the Creation Window by Painton Cowen,
David Gilliland and the Grimshaw/Costeloe Studio
Doves image (page 10) by Susanne Lin Jensen
Henri Matisse (page 26) courtesy of George Braziller, Inc.
All illustrations by Rosalind Grimshaw

Printed in Italy
The publishers have made every effort to ensure the accuracy of the
information in the book at the time of going to press. However, they cannot
accept any responsibility for any loss, injury or inconvenience resulting from
the use of information contained in this work.

Contents

"I started in stained glass from painting. My paintings, particularly after living in Africa, were increasingly about light or windows. The move to stained glass seemed logical because of its three very individual characteristics:

Looking at the images on the glass the colour is very intense.

Looking through glass the view is altered by the glass but still visible and significant.

The light shining through the glass varies with the hour and seasons, making the window almost an organic object, casting colours and illuminating the place it is in."

Ros Grimshaw

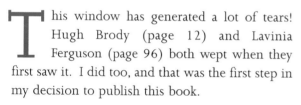

A story worth telling

by
Alastair Sawday

This window has generated a lot of tears! Hugh Brody (page 12) and Lavinia Ferguson (page 96) both wept when they first saw it. I did too, and that was the first step in my decision to publish this book.

I lived in Ros Grimshaw's house in the '70s, a small part of the chaotic, creative jumble that was her life even then. I would later see her walk past my window on the way home from work; then I would see her limp past, more and more markedly. When I popped in out of the blue to see her two years ago I was unprepared for 'the window'.

I saw only a collage of photos on the wall of Ros's hall. Not since I first saw Michelangelo's David had I wept at the sight of a work of art. Then, seeing Ros, who was in a 'kinetic' condition at the end of her day, I was suddenly taken by one of those mad inspirations: I am a publisher — should I not do a book to celebrate this window, this woman, this wonderful story? Even better, my childhood friend, Painton Cowen, was about to return to writing. He knew Ros and had once written and photographed two glorious books about Rose Windows and Stained Glass. The answer to my own question, therefore, was an immediate 'yes'.

The story in this book is grand yet domestic, involving a splendid cast of characters: carers, her partner Patrick, craftspeople, doctors, nurses, clergy, family, friends and neighbours. At the centre of it all is Ros, ill with Parkinson's yet an inspiration to all around her. It is not difficult, somehow, to imagine the crucial role of another guiding force.

I hope this book will touch you in many ways, as it has touched Rob Mackay, the designer. He too was inspired, both by the energy of the people involved and by the Creation Window itself. In rising to the challenge he has created another work of great beauty.

The central Creation story has inspired generations of us and can still do so, whatever our beliefs. At a time when much of our focus is on the future of our planet, speculation about its beginnings will not go away. Neither will our search for meaning.

Genesis, Chapter 1

"In the beginning God created the heaven and the earth.

And the earth was without form, and void; and darkness was upon the face of the deep.

And the spirit of God moved upon the face of the waters.

And God said, Let there be light: and there was light.

And God saw the light, that it was good: and God divided the light from the darkness.

And God called the light Day, and the darkness he called Night. And the evening and the morning were the first day".

Saturday 25th May 2002 - Bristol

5.40am
Outside it is dark with rain but the sun has risen. The bridge has just swung and a small but tall yacht is in the lock. I am eating grapes and thinking of subjects to mention to Painton, like a drawing or photos of the view; friends; recurring themes such as sun, moon, doves, fish.

6.30am
The sun changes. I am late in sorting out the drugs. These are critical to my function; without them I am inert matter.

The river is full and reflective.

My drug regime has been refined to this present cocktail over twenty years. I put today's drugs in a small Spanish inlaid-brass pillbox. I count out tomorrow's drugs into a round Tunisian one inlaid with brass and mother-of-pearl. There are 24 different tablets. I take three and a gingernut biscuit.

As my condition forces me to rise early, for many years now I have kept a dawn diary in photographic and drawn images. The Creation talks about evening, then morning, of the first day. These dawns are the only time I am alone, my own precious hours to write, draw and think; when the birds can be heard. There is a large flock of doves that fly below my window at dawn.

Foreword

by
Hugh Brody

The those of us who do not make art depend, for much of the light in our lives, on those who do. In my own homes, Rosalind Grimshaw's work has been everywhere – from delicate cut-outs pinned on the fridge to a painting in the bathroom. And she made a glowing, glorious piece for each of my children. At some point in every day, for many years, someone in my home has paused in front of art by Ros and taken delight, found nourishment from the way she transforms the light.

In 1998 I began work on a new book. Although there seemed no reason for it, nothing in the book's outline or plan, I picked up a copy of the Old Testament and began reading Genesis. I thought I knew it – and remembered having to learn chunks of it at Hebrew classes as a child. To my amazement, I found in it a meaning – an interpretation of the world – that was quite new to me. I then searched out a modern, scholarly translation, and discovered the work of Robert Alter. And I returned to the new book with a new, transforming idea. At about this point Ros phoned me. She wanted to talk about Genesis, and how to interpret some of its terms. She was eager to get hold of Alter's translation. She was working on an idea of a new window – not a commission, but a chance to tender for one: the new window at Chester Cathedral.

I was delighted rather than surprised by the coincidence of our engagement with Genesis. I had long felt that Ros was never very far away in spirit. And her brilliant, witty and persistent questioning of Genesis was as much an intellectual spur as it was companionship in the solitary business of writing. It also showed me something about the depth and range of Ros's way of working: she needed to know how specific Hebrew words had been translated and interpreted, how scholars had defined one or another part of the Genesis story, what everything might mean. She revealed her love of language and ideas – her need to understand everything in order to make a window.

Ros sent me a copy of her first set of ideas for the 12 panels – one large and one small for each day of Creation. They were hard to decipher, but from the beginning I saw an astonishing wealth of ideas. Later she sent some photographs of parts of the window as it took more definite form, and I began to see its inner glow, its beauty. Early this year, she and Patrick Costeloe sent me photographs of its being set in place, and I began to appreciate the scale of the achievement. Then, on July 26th 2001, I went to Chester for the window's dedication. In some, second-hand ways, I knew the window well – its size, structure, many of its details, its 'look' and the ideas from which it had grown. I was well prepared.

I arrived early and went to see the window an hour or so before the ceremony, to see for myself without the formality of a public occasion. As I walked toward the Cathedral, I saw the window from the outside. There was the shape, the scale, the leading. From the outside it was a pattern, a complex hint of the window's light. I walked down the stairs into the side door of the Cathedral and turned left into the space where the window dominates the end wall. I walked some distance into the room, not looking round, to get some distance away, to have a first, full view. The sun was shining, and even with my eyes to the ground I

skyscrapers to play to God's moment when he said 'let there be light'; or a medical scan of her own brain, the orb of her skull and the inside of her mind, to sit under the creation of the stars and the firmament above; or the African child in a flow of water to resonate with the birds and the fishes – life that depends on water. And achieved this wonderful exploration of ideas in a work that was, above all else, a thing of beauty – a glorious transformation of the light.

I had been looking at the window for some minutes before I noticed the Hand of God. There it was, across Creation. Then I looked at the wall, and saw a delicate pattern of white on the stone – God's fingers were projected there by the light. I realised that every bright day, as the sun moved across the window, the Hand of God would make its way across the Cathedral wall. The hand, and the window, and the work of Ros Grimshaw, forever there, in light, in and on the stone.

was aware of a soft glow of colour in the air and on the stones of the opposite wall. I stopped, turned, and took my first look. Within a few seconds, I realised that tears were running down my cheeks. The window was one of the most beautiful things I had ever seen.

For all the conversations about the ideas and glimpses I had been sent in the form of sketches and photographs, the window was astonishing – with a power and poignancy for which I was completely unprepared. I took time, I looked at each light, going from the evocations of the words of Genesis in the upper, large panels to their echoes in a 'real' or 'modern' world in the lower, small panels. I began to follow the play of light, images and thought: the brilliance of the art; the wonder of the thought inside the art. No one but Rosalind Grimshaw could have used the flow of night traffic and the window lights of

Preface

by
Painton Cowen

Stained glass windows are essentially about colour and communication - colour as communicated by natural transmitted light but changed by passing through the glass. They and the 'message' that they contain in their imagery are designed to impact, inform and delight the eye and mind of the beholder. Colour and impact have always been the hallmark of Rosalind Grimshaw's stained glass work. In 1983 she discovered that she had Parkinson's disease. Until then she had been a distinguished designer, artist and creator of stained glass windows - as well as mother of three. Since then, despite numerous difficulties, she has become even more distinguished, her immense activity culminating in her largest and, to many people, her finest window to date, the Creation Window in Chester. Ros has refused to let her illness prevent her from working. She says that the challenge has, paradoxically, brought about an intensely creative period in her life - if not the most creative in her entire career. The large window in the Refectory of the Cathedral in Chester – nearly 20 foot wide and over 15 foot high – shows a profound insight into the theme of the Creation and what it means in the new millennium. For each of the six 'Days' of The Creation as recounted in Genesis, displayed in the main lights, there is a scene below that is relevant to the world of today and tomorrow. The window serves as a reminder that The Creation is an ongoing process in which man's responsibility in all his ventures amid the planet's precarious future becomes more pronounced as the years go by.

In this book we trace the evolution of the window from the first sketches submitted in the year 2000 through acceptance of Ros's proposal to the Service of Dedication of the completed window in the Cathedral. The window was designed and made mostly at Ros's home in Bristol with her partner Patrick Costeloe - apart from six weeks

"The deeper he (the artist) looks, the more readily he can extend his view from the present to the past, the more deeply he is impressed by the one essential image of creation itself, Genesis, rather than by the image of nature, the finished product.

Then he permits himself the thought that the process of creation can today hardly be complete and he sees the act of world creation stretching from the past to the future. Genesis eternal!"

Paul Klee

14

when she was forced to be in hospital. Ros's admiration for the hospital staff knows no bounds; they helped her and her assistant Carrie convert her room on the ward into a design studio for that period. This stage in the window's evolution is an eye-opener to many of us - how to transform a potentially depressing time into a creative experience. Many contributed and all gained. The ward will never be the same again!

Ros kept a diary over the three months when the window was being made, including a series of charming sketches that described the work of the previous day together with comments and thoughts. Much of this is reproduced in this book. At the same time, a photographic record was made of the progress of the project. We see the huge life-size designs made from collage, the process of producing the 'cut lines', selecting and cutting the glass, connecting all the glass pieces with lead into panels and finally water-proofing them. The diary also records the comings and goings of friends and acquaintances as family life continues around the creation of the Creation Window.

Chester cathedral, alas, has no stained glass from the Middle Ages. Until the installation of the Millennium Creation Window in 2001 its windows were an assortment of 19th- and 20th-century stained glass with a fine display of early 20th-century glass in the cloisters. More recent glass includes Carter Shapland's huge and somewhat brooding heavy west window with its figures and symbols set against a deep blue background, glazed in 1961, as well as Alan Younger's mildly 'explosive' trio of Westminster Windows of 1992 in the nave. However, Rosalind Grimshaw's 21st-century marvel in the Refectory plays with the light like no other window in the cathedral, possibly like no other in the country. It is a tour-de-force that utilises glasses of many different kinds and ages to illuminate The Creation as recounted by chapter one of Genesis. It also points to mankind's ever-increasing role and responsibility in the on-going process of the Creation that we call Evolution. It matches up in every way to what the cathedral asked for, namely "a work of art to be enjoyed" that has "meaning in itself which can be explained." This book is an attempt to explain the window, its making and its remarkable creator.

A Man that looks on glasse,
On it may stay his eye;
Or if he pleaseth, through it passe,
And then the heav'n espie.

George Herbert

16

The Dean writes...

I am delighted to be associated with the publication of this special book. The Creation Window in Chester Cathedral is a great tribute to the imaginative skill and personal courage of the artist. It was a joy to share with Rosalind Grimshaw in the whole project, and I shall always remember the privilege of seeing the work in progress when I visited her Bristol studio.

Given the arrangement of the stone mullions in the west window of the Refectory, which leaves no central light, the choice by Ros of the six days of creation as her theme was inspired; and the modern counterparts to the sextet, in the lower panels, are touching and relevant expressions of the basic scriptural subject of human existence in a world of potential beauty. The glorious and dramatic use of colour in the stained glass suggests the joyousness of God's vibrant activity in bringing his creation to birth. As a result the whole window, with its dominant symbols of the hand of God and the dove of his Spirit, shimmers and glows in the daylight, even when the sun is not shining through it!

Those two images of divinity are a potent reminder to me of God's presence and power in his world, breathing life into it and, despite the problems of human society, helping it to move onwards. But these icons also speak to me of God's new creation in Christ, and of the gifts which, through the Spirit, he has released for us to use and enjoy. Such gifts are wonderfully apparent in the making of the Creation Window, which is a celebration: of faith in a God who is accessible, of hope for the future of his creative world, and of a refining love which he makes possible among his people.

Stephen Smalley

First impressions of
The Creation Window
in Chester Cathedral

In the Refectory
12.45 pm, 22/12/2001

It is three days before Christmas and I am in the Cathedral. It is past noon and as visitors go about their lunch the clatter of plates, the buzz of conversation and the occasional mobile phone tell us very clearly that we are in the 21st century. Five hundred years ago silence would probably have accompanied the brothers as they ate their midday meal in the Abbey's refectory - or perhaps a Biblical reading or even a psalm sung to keep their minds concentrated on holy thoughts.

Above the 17th-century Mortlake Tapestry on the Refectory's west wall is the large six-light window filled with pristine, new, stained glass - a blaze of colour bursting through the worn pink sandstone. It is about to receive the full light of the midday sun as it moves away from the southern-most point of its travel across the sky and begins its afternoon of shining onto the exterior west-facing wall of the Refectory.

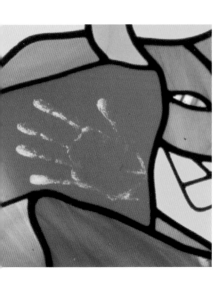

But even now the window is a riot of rich colour. The more one looks the more one sees: the rich and varied shapes give an initial impression of chaos - that is, before the mind and the eye discern the subtle order beneath the composition. And, indeed, that is the way things should be, since the subject of the window is The Creation, that incredible moment when Order was created from Chaos. The six lights define the six 'Days' as described by Genesis. Hovering across the four central lights is the white dove of The Spirit, whilst the Hand of God as a thin line interweaves the activity of the Days of Creation.

But the eye then notes that the Hand of God reaches across only five of the lights: the sixth light, representing the Creation of Mankind, has a small hand that seems to be reaching out towards God's Hand, reminiscent of Michelangelo's scene in the roof of the Sistine Chapel. One hand is giving, the other receiving. This gives much food for thought as one finishes the excellent lunch provided by the Cathedral catering staff.

Atop the window amid the Perpendicular tracery are the Sun and Moon, as in so many of the 15th-century windows, symbolising Night and Day. Also here are the Greek letters Alpha and Omega, symbols of The Creator: "I am Alpha and Omega, the First and the Last..." as St. John's Revelation declares it. After the hand and the dove it is probably the large red figure of the Leviathan -

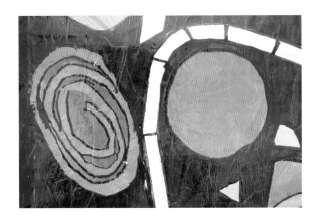

with his prismatic teeth and grinning out of the deep - that captures the attention. No sooner has one detected Leviathan than other fish around it, created here from exotic multicoloured glass, swim into view; and so, too, the birds above the great beast avoid his jaws or sit on the cliffs at a safe distance. Then the eye is perhaps drawn again to Man's hand in its orangy-red - which seems to be man-sized, and in fact is, although 'woman-sized' would be more accurate as I later learned that it was a 'shadow' of the glazier Rosalind Grimshaw's own hand. Somewhere, one thinks, one has seen that hand before …. in the pictures of caveman art … at Lascaux? It is the nearby red-orange bull and its horns that stimulate this echo of man's first attempts at art - deep in the bowels of the earth as mankind emerged from the Ice Ages.

As the eye roves around the window, it sees other familiar objects: flowers, fruit, grasses, people, planets, stars - and what seems like a view of the earth from space - which it is! A few words on the window are provided by the Cathedral authorities on a sheet of paper, so one can now confirm what one had guessed a few moments before: yes, it is a foetus, and - good heavens! - it is a brain scan, the glazier's own Parkinsonian brain we learn. There are butterflies, a pump, the Space Shuttle, a river estuary, lightning, galaxies, seeds……

But my thoughts and observations are interrupted by a change that is happening. It has just gone one o'clock and the sun is filling the panes with light: it is beginning to flood in and already the transmitted light is setting the stone mullions between the glass panels of the Days on fire. The long white lines of God's Hand are splitting the light into three, so that everywhere one line becomes three, Trinity-like. Over on the side wall, about ten feet away, little white dots appear - apparently from the individual panels that make up the big white dove, each one becoming a prism with carefully cut bevels in the glass. A few minutes later this wall bursts into colour, mingling pink-red the stone with the sharp of the rays of the sun that throws every colour from the window at it. As the minutes pass, everything intensifies as the sun gradually moves across the glass. The prisms from the dove are now throwing little five-pointed stars onto the long thin stone mullions between the lights. Even some of the lunchers look up from their plates and momentarily cease talking to their neighbours, amazed by this little miracle that is going on over their heads.

A few moments of reflection on this spectacle and I realise that I am witnessing a very special moment in time for this window. The winter solstice, around December 21st, is when the sun is at its lowest point in the sky during the year at midday. Whatever light and colour the window projects is then at its highest and most auspicious point on the wall inside the building. As the year passes this (light show) will get gradually lower each lunchtime. Around Easter the sun will be too high and the projections therefore too low and probably get 'lost' in the Refectory serving area - even among the lunchers themselves. But other effects may arise later in the day when the sun moves from west to north-west at midsummer and gets lower in the sky towards the end of the day: this will throw long colours onto the south wall - or so I guess! The answer will be to keep visiting Chester on sunny days throughout the year and see the surprises that this remarkable Creation Window has in store for us all.

The King James translation of Genesis

1 In the beginning God created the heaven and the earth.

2 And the earth was without form, and void; and darkness was upon the face of the deep. And the spirit of God moved upon the face of the waters.

3 And God said, Let there be light: and there was light.

4 And God saw the light, that it was good: and God divided the light from the darkness.

5 And God called the light Day, and the darkness he called Night. And the evening and the morning were the first day.

6 And God said, Let there be a firmament in the midst of the waters, and let it divide the waters from the waters.

7 And God made the firmament, and divided the waters which were under the firmament from the waters which were above the firmament: and it was so.

8 And God called the firmament Heaven. And the evening and the morning were the second day.

9 And God said, Let the waters under the heaven be gathered together unto one place, and let the dry land appear: and it was so.

10 And God called the dry land Earth; and the gathering together of the waters called he Seas: and God saw that it was good.

11 And God said, Let the earth bring forth grass, the herb yielding seed, and the fruit tree yielding fruit after his kind, whose seed is in itself, upon the earth: and it was so.

12 And the earth brought forth grass, and herb yielding seed after his kind, and the tree yielding fruit, whose seed was in itself, after his kind: and God saw that it was good.

13 And the evening and the morning were the third day.

14 And God said, Let there be lights in the firmament of the heaven to divide the day from the night; and let them be for signs, and for seasons, and for days, and years:

15 And let them be for lights in the firmament of the heaven to give light upon the earth: and it was so.

16 And God made two great lights; the greater light to rule the day, and the lesser light to rule the night: he made the stars also.

17 And God set them in the firmament of the heaven to give light upon the earth,

18 *And to rule over the day and over the night, and to divide the light from the darkness: and God saw that it was good.*

19 *And the evening and the morning were the fourth day.*

20 *And God said, Let the waters bring forth abundantly the moving creature that hath life, and fowl that may fly above the earth in the open firmament of heaven.*

21 *And God created great whales, and every living creature that moveth, which the waters brought forth abundantly, after their kind, and every winged fowl after his kind: and God saw that it was good.*

22 *And God blessed them, saying, Be fruitful, and multiply, and fill the waters in the seas, and let fowl multiply in the earth.*

23 *And the evening and the morning were the fifth day.*

24 *And God said, Let the earth bring forth the living creature after his kind, cattle, and creeping thing, and beast of the earth after his kind: and it was so.*

25 *And God made the beast of the earth after his kind, and cattle after their kind, and every thing that creepeth upon the earth after his kind: and God saw that it was good.*

26 *And God said, Let us make man in our image, after our likeness: and let them have dominion over the fish of the sea, and over the fowl of the air, and over the cattle, and over all the earth, and over every creeping thing that creepeth upon the earth.*

27 *So God created man in his own image, in the image of God created he him; male and female created he them.*

28 *And God blessed them, and God said unto them, Be fruitful, and multiply, and replenish the earth, and subdue it: and have dominion over the fish of the sea, and over the fowl of the air, and over every living thing that moveth upon the earth.*

29 *And God said, Behold, I have given you every herb bearing seed, which is upon the face of all the earth, and every tree, in the which is the fruit of a tree yielding seed; to you it shall be for meat.*

30 *And to every beast of the earth, and to every fowl of the air, and to every thing that creepeth upon the earth, wherein there is life, I have given every green herb for meat: and it was so.*

31 *And God saw every thing that he had made, and, behold, it was very good. And the evening and the morning were the sixth day.*

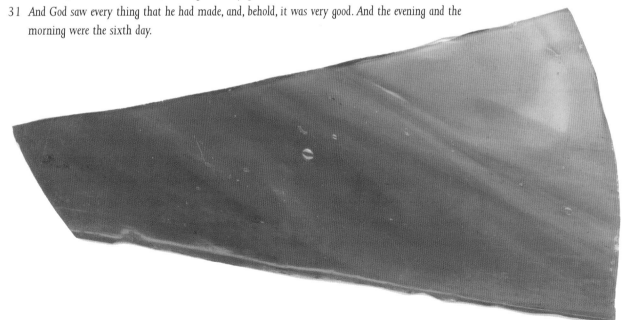

" ...We want to affirm that in all progress and development, spiritual, social and cultural, God is there, enabling change, even if His hand in it is not always perceived."......

"Our preferred view is that an abstract design should be used to depict the main theological themes, rather than detailed images, and that bold colours should be used..."

"The design needs to stand on its own, so that the window will be a work of art to be enjoyed. But it also needs to have a meaning in itself, which can be explained: reflecting the permanence of God in Christ (the same yesterday, today and for ever), as well as denoting His energy and openness to the future through the Spirit."

From the design brief for Chester Cathedral's Millennium Stained Glass Window

"The world is a book, written by the finger of God"

Hugh of St Victor, 12th century

An introduction to Genesis in the new Millennium

The message of The Creation Window

"In the beginning God created the heaven and the earth…" Thus begins the first chapter of Genesis in the Bible, possibly the most widely read book – and probably the most widely read passage – of all time. Genesis has been translated, re-translated, interpreted, explained and re-interpreted by thousands of scholars over the centuries. Many think that it has now been satisfactorily 'explained-away' and replaced by the latest theories of cosmology and evolution; but – whatever the case – its noble words still impress our 'sophisticated' minds today at the dawn of the third millennium, over 2,500 years after they were written down.

The spiritual truths of the Genesis account refuse to lie down. We can make allowances for the vocabulary, language and imagery, yet still a central message comes through. Fast-advancing science cannot dispel it. Science confirms that the heavens and the earth were created in an instant, in the Big Bang. Light was indeed the first 'element' created, just as the Bible says.

Doubtless every reader of Genesis derives his or her own message from the text, but there is,

I suggest, one universal 'message' that Rosalind Grimshaw has captured in this remarkable window. The subject is the Six 'Days' of Creation. She was guided by a translation of Genesis by Robert Alter rather than the more familiar King James version. Alter, a professor of Hebrew at the University of California, has studied the nuance of every word and phrase and the outcome is essentially the Genesis we all know and love but with subtle insights that add another aspect to the more familiar account. This version is used for the accounts of the Creation in this book.

The implication in all accounts of Genesis is that God created the heavens and the earth in six days and then 'rested' on the seventh. Man had been created on the sixth day – or as Alter translates it, "the human" was then created, and both accounts add emphatically "*in His own image*". This phrase has caused as much debate as any in Genesis, but the implications are clear from what follows in the Genesis account. Mankind was entrusted with looking after the earth, but acting under God's guidance.

As all the world knows, this initial plan went disastrously wrong when Adam and Eve disobeyed God's command and ate the fruit of the Tree of

Beneath the Creation of Light (1st day) is portrayed Man lighting the darkness of night through artificial light.

Beneath the Creation of the Firmament (2nd day) is a view of the Earth from the space Shuttle.

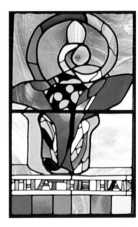

Beneath the Creation of Trees and Grasses (3rd Day) is a portrayal of the science of pollination.

"The traditional purpose of stained glass was always to tell stories and this is an aspect I still cherish, but I want them to be told slowly over a period of time; each time the window is looked at a little more is revealed."

Ros Grimshaw

Knowledge. They discovered they were 'naked', were cast out of the Garden of Eden and thus cut off from God's continuing moment-by-moment Grace: that is, from the ability to discern His Knowledge, His Wisdom and the power to resist evil, other than by choice and their own efforts.

In the world, Adam and Eve and their descendants – we that is – are destined to work for a living, to struggle, to suffer but also to live our lives as we choose or as circumstances allow us to. We still have the capacity to love, to experience joy, to exercise free will. Above all, we may choose to look to God for Knowledge, Wisdom and the guidance that otherwise eludes us in our 'fallen' state. Much of the Old Testament recounts how Adam's descendants struggle with this situation, and whether we regard much of the Old Testament as fact, elaborated fact, fiction, mythology or a mixture of all of these things, the promise of Free Will remains to this day: we can go it alone or invite God into our lives, which in Christianity is achieved by a belief in the permanence of God in Christ.

In Rosalind's window this 'handing over' to Man on the sixth day is interpreted literally. The Hand of God, that can be seen in the window to cover the first five days, only extends towards the sixth, whilst in the sixth window itself a disembodied hand is portrayed reaching out to God's Hand – reminiscent of the celebrated scene in the Vatican's Sistine Chapel where God reaches out to Adam – who limply responds.

Both of these scenes, at Chester and at the Vatican, symbolise the gift from The Creator to Mankind not only of Life, but also of Creativity itself: an invitation to become nothing less than a co-creator with God. The Spirit, that continues to underpin the whole of Creation and the laws of Physics is the same Spirit that "hovered over the waters" before the First Day of Creation in Genesis. It is now offered to Man. It enables man to love to the full as well as to create works of great beauty. It is now up to mankind to play its part in the evolution of the world in a way that makes sense – but at the moment we seem to be making rather a mess of it!

24

Beneath the Creation of Stars and Planets (4th day) is a representation of 'inner space' as opposed to 'outer space' in the form of Ros's own brain scan.

Beneath the Creation of Birds and Fish (5th Day) is a pump, symbolising the importance of acquiring water in the modern world with environmentally sensitive – rather than destructive – technology.

Beneath the Creation of Man (6th Day) is a picture of a foetus in the womb. Above the foetus are a pair of DNA spirals and beneath it the twin serpents, symbolising medicine – but also a caduceus, an ancient symbol of knowledge and, ultimately, knowledge of Good and Evil.

Our own lives and the lives of others can be changed for the better. All true artists worthy of the title are, I believe, pursuing The Truth in their art through their total commitment of mind, body and soul in every moment of their creativity. In so doing, whether they know it or not, they are doing God's work, since work at its highest is Love-in-action. The same is true of *any* other activity that is pursued in like manner. The Spirit of Truth and Love is present whenever it is truly sought – whenever our 'hand' reaches out in total sincerity.

In this series of windows the six 'Days' of Creation are portrayed according to the description in the Bible for each of those days. In the lower panels (*above*) is a series of six panels that relate those above to today's, and to tomorrow's world.

The message from these lower panels and particularly from the last one is abundantly clear – almost frighteningly so. Man's powers are already almost god-like: we have the technical possibility of 'designer' babies and of transforming Nature for our convenience and for our profit. The responsibilities and consequences for future generations are awesome.

The knowledge that man's powers can be used for Good or Evil has pervaded every culture since the beginning of civilisation, but now the reality of that power bewilders us. In using that power humanity needs all the Wisdom and Knowledge that God gives – and all the receptivity that Man is capable of attaining in order to hear and transmit it.

All that is needed for any person to begin to move in the direction of Truth and Love are five things: genuine Concern, real Courage, total Commitment, an enlivened Consciousness and knowing how to open oneself to the Knowledge and Wisdom of The Creator himself. A work of great beauty and filled with meaning and wisdom can help and inspire us to make a start at any point in our lives. The Creation Window at Chester is just such a work.

Telling it in pictures

by Patrick Costeloe

Henri Matisse at work

1952 A black and white photograph of a man. His beard and any last wisps of hair are white; otherwise he is bald and bespectacled. He is seated and holds a pair of scissors in one hand...

2000 A colour photograph of a woman, seated and at work in front of a twelve-foot high drawing board. She has scissors in her hand, and, like shards of glass, coloured paper offcuts at her bare feet.

Having tried to draw up a cartoon in pastels and feeling it did not convey the sense of the finished window, Rosalind decided to do all the full-size drawings of the stained glass in *papier collé*.

The practical decision to execute the full-size colour cartoons for the Chester Cathedral commission using this technique proved to be a revelation. Cutting into dyed and coloured paper is an effective way of designing, realising and showing what a finished stained glass window will look like. The rawness of cutting into sheets of coloured paper is as close to cutting sheets or pieces of glass as can be. It also gives the artist a continuing reference for how much glass will be needed – the shapes in paper mirroring the glass needed. The decisions in the colour also rehearse and fix what is already in the artist's mind when she comes to look for and buy the glass needed for the commission.

The original design for the whole project was done like this. The translation of the full-size cartoons into cut and leaded glass was a critical and inspirational step from the artist's original idea to the finished artwork. Those vast cartoons were, however, partly a response to the urgency of the project.

The initial invitation to submit designs was made in April 2000, in a limited competition of four designers. By May 2000 it was to be a shortlist of two designers out of the four, with a final decision as to the chosen design by the end of June 2000. As it turned out one of the four designers invited dropped out so the initial pool was three.

At the first stage of this selection process Rosalind's design was deemed to be so exciting and inspirational to the Dean and Chapter that the shortlist became irrelevant. The 'go ahead' was decided and the project was given the 'all stations go'... except for the final agreement of the CFCE (Cathedrals' Fabric Commission for England) which would not meet till September 2000.

Given that the commission had to be completed by June 2001 – and that the windows are 165 square foot of stained glass, there was no practical way to invest in the glass or provide the finance needed for other participators in the project till the final CFCE agreement was reached. Because of this it was agreed with the Dean and Chapter of Chester Cathedral that the artist could move forward with full-scale drawings, which they would pay for, to put the artist in a position of maximum readiness for the day of the final 'go ahead'.

In effect, the Dean and Chapter funded templates being made on site, drawing boards and trays in which to set out the glass, paper, pencils, dyes, and Rosalind's time up to this point.

This delay turned out to be something of a blessing since the period between the award of the commission and its final 'green light go ahead' (June-July 2000) saw Rosalind go into hospital for a major readjustment for her Parkinson's disease treatment. The initial designs had already seized the imagination and excitement of the commissioners of the project as well as all our friends and family. Like the proverbial pebble in a pool the ripple was spreading. It saw Rosalind take over the hospital rehabilitation wards where she was an inspirational figure to many as she carried on with her collages. Patients, nurses, doctors, friends, family visited this hospital room which was now also an artist's workshop.

And this is the heart of the matter. Rosalind has been diagnosed with Parkinson's disease for twenty years now but is able to batter at the condition through her art. The limitations are not just overcome but overcome in such a way that the words 'ability' or 'disability' become unhelpful. What I am describing is a deeply frustrating predicament that leaves existence in a very raw, flayed state.

There is an extraordinary essay written about painting from the painter's point of view by RB Kitaj. It is the introduction to an exhibition of paintings he

"The Parkinson's condition means that the person who suffers from it is subjected to uncoordinated movements. Ros's hand takes off, seizes a piece of glass like an eagle swooping down onto its prey, and spinning motions take the arm to an unlikely destination – but miraculously the piece of glass, like water being dropped from an aircraft onto a forest fire, finds its right place in the complex scheme. Patrick Costeloe, her supporter, friend and partner, will later lead the pieces of glass together and realise other technical aspects of the composition."
Meeting with Rosalind Grimshaw, by Régis Gal

Dyed paper strips for the collage hang out to dry.

selected from The National Gallery Collection in 1980. The title of the exhibition was *The Painter's Eye*. The kernel of the essay is the idea of vision. He states his love and admiration of the paintings by Titian, Rembrandt and Monet in their old age. What they all had in common was humanity, compassion, an understanding of beauty and very long lives. What they also had in common was a lifetime of art, painting and encroaching blindness, and that the paintings considered their greatest are those produced at the end of their lives... when their sight was weakest but their skills and vision were greatest.

The artist, Henri Matisse, has been a recurrent theme through the Chester Cathedral project. The collage technique Rosalind used was inspired by Matisse's book *Jazz* and *The Cut-outs of Henri Matisse* by John Elderfield. Matisse designed the chapel at Vence, including the stained glass, as a 'thank you' to the nuns who nursed him back to health after a grave illness. Matisse saw art as essentially joyful. Rosalind insisted that at no point should there be anything other than Joy in her Creation window. Matisse was such an influence on Rosalind that she put a 'quarry' with the design of one of the Vence windows into the Creation Window.

June 2001 Fitting the windows. 'El momento de verdad' is what bullfighters call it, a moment that is

both seconds and eternity. In this case the moment is two weeks. The transport, and the steady slog of taking out the existing windows and then...

The fixing team are filmed for a whole afternoon by Granada Television. They film the panels measured on the ground, the designs all laid out, three different angle shots of fitting a panel, interviews with all the fixing team... the film must come to at least half an hour. The window is explained, the commentator's hand describing with a sweep the panel that depicts flowers, vegetables and fruits and the 'diamond' of Matisse's St Paul de Vence chapel windows – it can't be seen from the ground, but that doesn't mean it isn't there.

1952 A black and white photograph of a man, his beard and any last wisps of hair are white, otherwise he is bald and bespectacled. He is seated and holds a pair of scissors in one hand, the piece of paper he cuts in the other. Around his bare feet, on the floor lie black and white pools of paper off cuts. The chair the man sits in is a wheelchair. Obviously the man is an artist. Just as obviously, he is crippled, unable to walk, disabled. Is this what he is or is he... Henri Matisse?

Description of the window

Ros's description:
"I have tried to show the continuous miracle of creation in its variety and richness, and the miracle of the sun rising every morning."

Above and around the Six Days

The Holy Spirit, portrayed as a large white dove and spread across the four central panels, descends from the Vaults of Heaven, symbolised by the Sun and Moon, the Greek letters Alpha and Omega and a collection of multi-coloured square quarries. The dove is created from 82 clear diamond-shaped quarries that are, in fact, prisms with bevelled edges on the inside surfaces. When the sun shines onto the window these prisms project stars onto the adjacent stone mullions that separate the Six Days (see the book jacket). The dove represents "the Spirit of God hovering over the waters", as described in Genesis: it is ever present in daily life sustaining Nature and the Cosmos.

Immediately beneath the dove are more of the quarries of the Vaults of Heaven that continue round the whole window forming the border; they symbolise the space between God and His Creation that surrounds and includes everything in the Cosmos. The colours of these pieces are variations on the basic colours that Ros used in the collage paper that formed the design: saffron, indigo, turquoise, purple, mint, ochre and 'madder' red.

In one of these 'quarries' – above the Delta in Day 2 – can be seen Ros's tribute to the great artist Henri Matisse: a tiny replica of one of the windows in the chapel at Vence.

In another quarry in the left hand border can be seen the initials of many of the people who contributed to the window in some way or other.

Each 'Day' of the Creation is contained within one of the six main openings – called 'lights' – within the window. At the top of the First and Sixth Days, just below the curved border, are two angels: the angel above mankind reminds us that mankind was, originally, created "a little lower than the angels" as it says in Psalm 8.

The Hand of God stretches right across the first five Days. It is a favourite motif of Ros's; she uses it regularly in the Advent calendars that she designs and makes in stained glass. Here, the white line is created by a succession of long thin rectangular-shaped pieces of bevelled glass. The effect is to almost 'focus' the light, or at least to ensure that the Hand of God is always visible – even into the late evening when the light fails and the other details in the window are all but lost. When the sun shines through the window (i.e. soon after noon) these bevelled pieces act as prisms and split the light into three thin rays (see the photograph on the book jacket).

The world is charged with the grandeur of God.
It will flame out, like shining from shook foil,
It gathers to a greatness like the ooze of oil
Crushed. Why do men then now not reck His rod?
Generations have trod, have trod, have trod;
     And all is seared with trade; bleared, smeared with toil;
     And bears man's smudge, and shares man's smell; the soil
Is bare now, nor can foot feel being shod.
And for all this, nature is never spent;
     there lives the dearest freshness deep down things;
And though the last lights from the black west went,
     Oh, morning at the brown brink eastwards springs -
Because the Holy Ghost over the bent
     World broods with warm breast, and with, ah, bright wings.

Gerald Manley Hopkins

Day 1

AND GOD SAW

Main window
The Creation of Light
and division of light and dark

Ros's description:

The upper and outer left-hand light is darkness and light and the Spirit of God shown as an eagle. Most of the lower lights have a scientific connection. The lower and outer left-hand light is taken from an image of skyscrapers at night photographed on a long time exposure so the car headlights and rear lights become coloured lines.

At the very top is an angel with yellow face (the other angel at the top of Day 6 is pink) and a yellow and white nimbus. The wings are, appropriately, made with lovely 'Angel Glass', i.e. streaky gold-pink American opaque glass with whitish patches.

The feeling in the main window is ultimately that of the heat of Creation but at the beginning – at the top – it is a 'crystal cold' blue arctic sky. A pair of binoculars might reveal that the centre of the star at the top is in fact a Swedish glass 'coaster' of the 1960s! The Aurora Borealis is just below the star in streaky purple glass set against the dark blue night sky...

"Imagine the crystal darkness of an arctic night, a canopy of stars and a glowing arc of aurora, the northern lights", says Hugh Brody, author of *The Other Side of Eden.*

As the eye moves down the window, so the mood moves from ice-cold Arctic towards the heat of the Creation. The dawn sky emerges from the blue – the white/yellow oval-shaped piece has a thin sliver of streaky purple again: this is inspired by the dawn view from Windsor Terrace that greets Ros every morning. Here the words "Let There Be Light" come to life for Ros – the miracle of life is re-affirmed with each new day.

Out of this dawn sky emerges a thunderstorm; this produces the lightning that extends right down to the eagle at the bottom of the main window. The reds and browns that make up much of the forming earth are interspersed with lightning in opalescent blue glass. This streaks down in thin filaments from the dark night sky through the forming earth. There is lots of 'plating' here – that is, putting two or more sheets of glass together, one on top of the other. This gives an added effect of variety and richness within the glass. Much of this is carried out with English glass – streaky yellow, gold-pink glass behind streaky browns and streaky reds for the 'storm' effect. Browns and orange dominate the middle panels, through which some 'shadows' of the lightning pieces can be seen in the thin pieces of sinew-like lead that is soldered onto the surface of the underlying glass.

The lightning is also symbolised in a small flashed-red piece of American glass that, by chance, looks like a swan just below the white line of the sleeve of The Hand of God and above the eagle (see photo on right). The Dunne-Za Indians of North West America believed that the swan caused the lightning.

Day 1

When God began to create heaven and earth, and the earth then was welter and waste and darkness over the deep and God's breath hovering over the waters, God said, "Let there be light." And there was light. And God saw the light, that it was good, and God divided the light from the darkness. And God called the light Day, and the darkness He called Night. And it was evening and it was morning, first day.

33

And God said Let there be light: and there was Light.

The grey-blue eagle at the bottom of the light represents The Spirit of God. The glass from which it is made has much acid etching (see the account for May 11-13 in the diary section). The purply glass just above the eagle is 'Angel Wing' glass again, the American opaque streaky pink and white; here it represents "God's breath hovering over the waters". Below the eagle is the 'black' glass that is, in fact, an 'old' piece of deep mauve glass from the stained glass firm Joseph Bell & Son, where Ros and Patrick learned much of their trade. This piece of glass had been inadvertently partially acided and this had dulled part of the surface. Nevertheless when the fierce light of the sun gets behind this glass the effect looks just wonderful as the deep mauve emerges from the 'black'

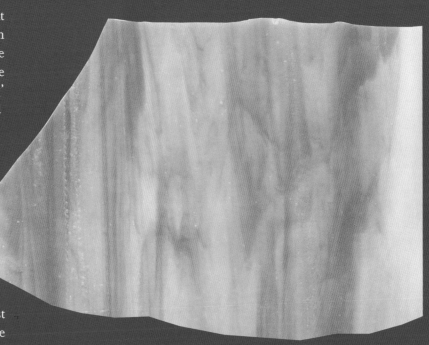

The choice of the eagle here as "God's breath", was influenced by the translation by the Hebrew scholar Robert Alter whose footnote indicated that the wingbeat of an eagle is hinted at here in the Hebrew. Also, the eagle is the symbol or emblem of St John, author of the Gospel that begins with the words "In the beginning was the Word": the parallel between the Breath of God and the Word of God is unmistakable. Also Dean Smalley, in memory of whose retirement and his services to Chester Cathedral this window was given, is a scholar who has specialised in the Gospel of St John.

LEFT: part of the exhibition collage

Day 1

Lower window
This represents mankind lighting the darkness.

Lights created by traffic coming (white) and going (red) and some turning off (yellow) appear as long streaks in a photographic time exposure. Behind are skyscrapers at night, interspersed with flashes of light from cameras.

Behind the lights created by traffic and skyscrapers is more of the 'black' glass. The translucent 'terrazzi' squares – generally used for bathrooms, pools etc – here become sky scrapers at night! In the very bottom left of the border here is a single terrazzi panel – this is Ros's homage to the artist Paul Klee who performed many experiments often with square blocks of colours when he was at the Bauhaus in the 1920s.

The 'flashes of light' from cameras are 'fused stars' of glass, specially made for Ros by Jane Jewson, Mike Slaughter's partner at Messrs. Creative Glass in Bristol.

The leading of this panel was a real challenge for Patrick. (See photograph on left.) Ros says it was also complicated and difficult to draw, design and cut. The pink streaks here include the very expensive flashed gold-pink glass, cut as long strips. (This glass is also used elsewhere in the window for fish, birds, the big flower and the woman's dress in Day 5.) A sharp-eyed observer will note other pinks and purples, blue, brown and orange streaks.

Ros originally designed this window in pastels before doing the collage.

Ros adds: "This window not only shows mankind's control of electricity, but also the fantastic new vision that photography has given to us."

Day 2

EVERYTHING

Ros's description
The upper and inner left-hand light shows a river estuary
as water reaches the sea and dry land appears. The lower
window shows the oceans of the earth as seen from the
Hubble Telescope when being visited by the Shuttle.

Main window
The Firmament, Heaven and the Waters

There is a fine yellow Greek letter Alpha – A – in the very top tracery light: over in Day 5 at the same position is a similarly styled Omega – W. These two letters have, in Christian iconography, evolved into symbols that can be recognised at a glance. They are the first and last letters in the Greek alphabet and refer to the quotation in the Bible where Christ, as God, announces: "I am Alpha and Omega, the Beginning and the End, the First and the Last." (Revelation 22.13). Placing these two 'symbols' in this position in windows was very common in the stained glass windows of the Middle Ages.

The main subject is a river delta. The glass here is mostly blue and blue-pink. The pink element in the blue waters represents man-made pollution – as can be seen in photographs of certain estuaries taken from space. The deep blue colour is brought about by plating (see glossary) with various combinations of glass, of one streaky glass with another streaky, here creating a turquoise colour at the bottom. The banks of the delta are in dark grey American opaque glass, a more subdued colour that acts as an effective contrast to the richness of the waters in plated streaky blues. The channels in the delta also evoke a woman's hair and even a waterfall…..

RIGHT: aerial photo of a mineral stained river delta

Day 2

And God said, "Let there be a vault in the midst of the waters, and let it divide water from water." And God made the vault and it divided the water beneath the vault from the water above the vault, and so it was. And God called the vault Heavens, and it was evening and it was morning, second day.

39

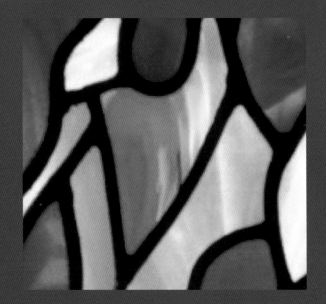

Note amongst the quarries in the tracery lights is a tiny tribute to Matisse – a sketch of one of his windows in the chapel at Vence, in the south of France (left). Viewers with 20/20 eyesight – or the rest of us with a pair of binoculars – will discern a pale blue quarry with a suggestion of a figure, a piece that became known in the studio as the 'ghost quarry'! (Page 40, bottom right). Jem, Ros's son made this and Esther, Ros's daughter, made a nearby quarry portraying a butterfly (page 39, bottom left). In the midst of the 'polluted waters' is a small red 'heart' of humanity (above), made from a piece of old glass recovered from a former window.

> The glazier "tries all his effects in the glass itself; he sketches in glass. He has all the colours burning round him, singing to him to use them, sounding all their chords. 'This looks better.' 'That is a pleasant harmony.' 'Ah! But this makes it sing!'"
>
> Christopher Whall

Lower window

A view of Earth from the Shuttle when visiting the Hubble telescope.

After exhaustive models attempting to represent the earth using many pieces of glass, Ros came across this single piece of magnificent blue and streaky-white glass some two feet across that catches perfectly the essence of that unique view. It was not quite large enough to do the whole scene in a single piece as can be seen by the lead line in the top right corner, where an additional piece was fitted in. The 'waviness' across the whole sheet's uneven surface can be seen as striations even with the naked eye. The tail fin of the Shuttle uses a piece of triangular shaped garish 'Gold Mirror' – iridescent green – glass. Two further triangular pieces line the Shuttle's green fins. The background here is very deep blue, almost black glass, evoking the blackness of outer space.

Day 3

THAT HE HAD

Ros's description
The upper and lower centre left-hand light has grasses and fruit showing their seeds. Below is the magnification of a butterfly egg on young plant tendrils and pollen being taken from a flower, representing an understanding of plants, their uses and the ability to feed the world.

Main window
Creation of Dry Land, grass, herbs, fruit and seeds

At the very top in the traceries is the 'Greater Light', the sun; next door in a similar position in Day 4 is a crescent moon. As with the nearby Alpha and Omega 'symbols' in this position at the top of the window, Ros is following a medieval tradition of placing the sun and moon up here at the top of the 'light'.

Ros says that this window took a lot of time to do! Hours were spent choosing just the right glass and it is rich in 'streakies' (see Glossary). It was surprisingly difficult to get a uniform dark blue background to all the fruit in the upper section of the upper light – and likewise the lighter blue in the lower section of the upper light.

The emphasis here is on seed-bearing plants, herbs and fruits. We can discern an apple, a slice of orange, a purply-mauve fig, a pink water-melon, a huge red and yellow pepper, a pumpkin, cereals and peas in pods (made of glass 'globs') as well as the leaves of some of these plants. Plated American 'Fracture and Streamers' glass is used in the seed sections of the melon, fig-leaf and pumpkin. The pumpkin is at the bottom right of the window, its seeds plated with a kind of orange-red glass.

Day 3

And God said, "Let the waters under the heavens be gathered in one place so that the dry land will appear," and so it was. And God called the dry land Earth and the gathering of waters He called Seas, and God saw that it was good. And God said, "Let the earth grow grass, plants yielding seed of each kind and trees bearing fruit of each kind, that has its seed within it." And so it was. And the earth put forth grass, plants yielding seed of each kind, and trees bearing fruit that has its seed within it of each kind, and God saw that it was good. And it was evening and it was morning, third day.

The magnificent large red, orange and yellow pepper is very striking. It was designed and made in a matter of a few hours after a friend had brought it to the studio. Ros says: "I was so struck by the beauty of it sitting there on the kitchen table. Also how appropriate it was at this point in the Creation story where seeds are playing such an important part: just look at those seeds!" This pepper is made with three grades of selenium glass: selenium red, selenium orange and selenium yellow.

The apples at the top of this window are exactly as they were in the garden at Windsor Terrace last autumn – red and juicy!

Grasses, wheat, bulrushes, herbs, peas and sweet peas all compete for space in the bottom section. The spiral tendril (below the fig) is a 'crown' of glass (see Glossary). The 'globs' for the peas came from an assorted collection of lumps, spheres and circular pieces of glass that Ros had amassed over the years.

Lower window
The theme is feeding the world

"Note the brown/green butterfly with a big orchid-like flower behind," says Ros, adding, "the beaker shape gives a hint of genetically modified foods." She acknowledges Paul Carter's help here with the butterfly and flower biology.

The glass for the butterfly was cut by an apprentice – Ros's next door neighbour's daughter, Alice Ferguson. The butterfly's egg, which looks a bit like a bishop's mitre, is a particularly fine piece of streaky-yellow glass. The spiral green tendril is, somewhat extravagantly, actually cut from a single piece of green/white crown of glass and then each piece plated with streaky in order to get just the right effect. The background is a streaky-yellow on green.

The beaker gives a hint of the science laboratory and within it is an impression of the way in which flower stems are seen through water in the glass. The flower itself is made from a rich thick piece of gold-pink glass – not made any more – that Ros spotted in the corner of the supplier's store-room. (It may even, before that, have come from another older studio). This lovely glass also appears in the dress of the woman washing the child (lower Day 5), and in strips in the lower panel of Day 1. "I could hardly bear to cut it!" confesses Ros.

Let the earth bring forth grass, the herb yielding seed, and the fruit tree yielding fruit after his kind

Day 4

MADE AND

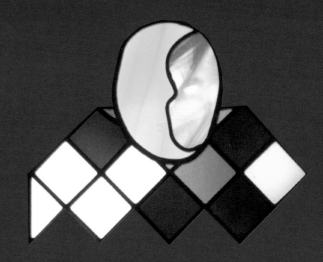

Ros's description

The upper and centre right-hand light shows the planets and universe of 'outer space' and their similarity to 'inner space' as shown in the lower and centre right-hand light which is a copy of a PET scan of my Parkinsonian brain.

Main window

Subject: The theme is outer space: the 'Lights in the firmament', planets, stars, galaxies, a comet . . . .

There is a certain artistic licence here in the composition of cosmos! A sharp eye will discern a purple galaxy with a hint of spiral form (inspired by Darcy Thompson's book *On Form in Nature*), Halley's Comet, a fiercely red Mars, crescent moons, planet 'Bow Tie', another bizarre pizza-like planet christened 'Packman' (with a slice missing!), a streaky-purple Jupiter and, to its left, a grey Saturn with its ring. At the very bottom is the top half of a large pale yellow sun in streaky glass of the 1930s with protruding flames in various colours generated by plating different glasses together. The glass for this piece came from the Bristol Guild when a window there was changed. The green earth is created from the bottom section of a bottle! Halley's Comet has a fine tail made from Bariolé glass (as are some of the fish in the next window).

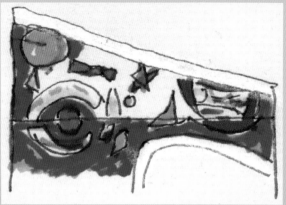

Day 4

And God said, "Let there be lights in the vault of the heavens to divide the day from the night, and they shall be signs for the fixed times and for days and years, and they shall be lights in the vault of the heavens to light up the earth." And so it was. And God made the two great lights, the great light for dominion of day and the small light for dominion of night, and the stars. And God placed them in the vault of the heavens to light up the earth and to have dominion over day and night and to divide the light from the darkness. And God saw that it was good. And it was evening and it was morning, fourth day.

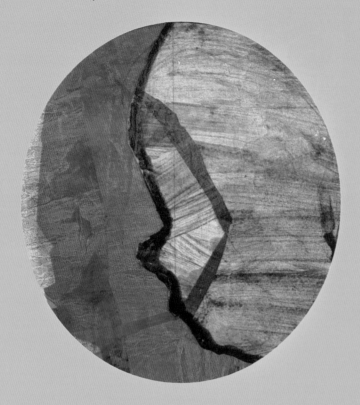

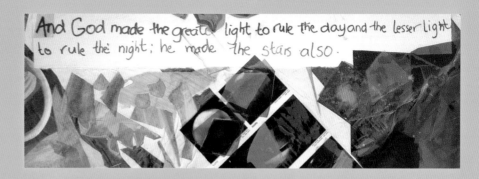

And God made the greater light to rule the day and the lesser light to rule the night; he made the stars also.

One 'planet' here is made from American green glass (originally destined for the peas in the previous window, but now in the cosmos as well as at the centre of planet Packman). All sorts of odds and ends are to be found here in this cosmos, some apparently awaiting discovery by man: some of them are even made from 'jewels' of glass with cut faces, acting as prisms.

There is an extraordinary 'angel' (below) at the top of the Cosmos – within the thumb of the Hand of God – made up from a mosaic of various pieces of glass all fused together – but then the composition was inadvertently dropped and had to be fused again: a kind of con-fused angel, one might say!

"Do things because you love them. If purple is your favourite colour, put purple in your window; if green, green, if yellow, yellow. Flowers and leaves and buds because you love them. Glass because you love it."

Christopher Whall

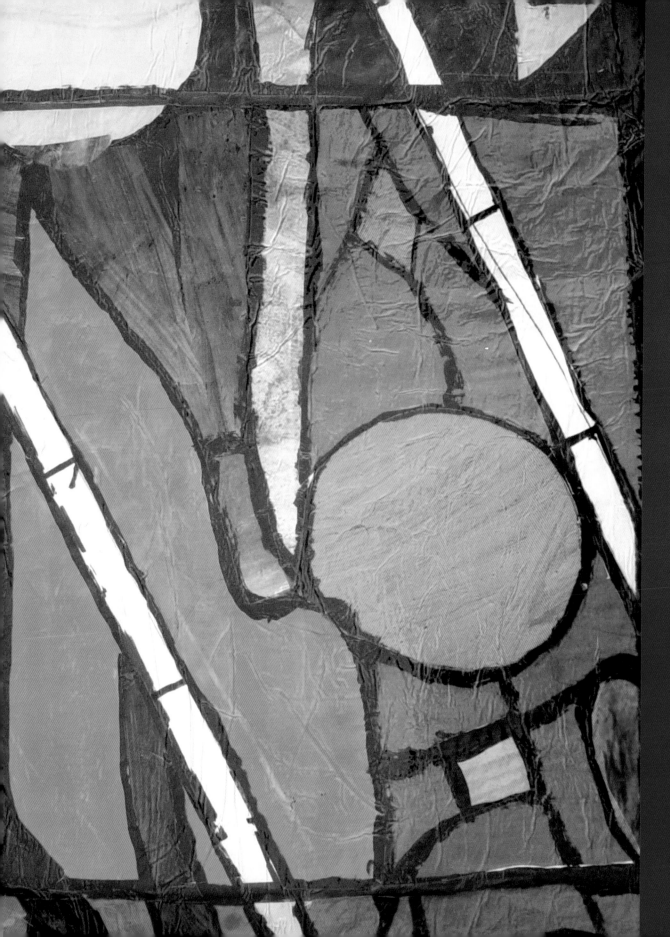

Lower window
Inner Space

This is an image of Ros's Parkinsonian brain, with its depleted dopamine. Here again a certain amount of artistic licence has been used as the colours are artificial and introduced into the design in order to make the image easier for the medical staff to see. It is a panel that has lots of Ros's favourite pieces of old glass that she had been putting aside for years, awaiting the right moment for their use – and here they are, old purple round the edge and gold-pink on blue glass. The main body of the brain, as it were, is one sheet of old flashed blue on yellow glass – a collector's item piece that gives the appearance of having faded from dark blue to light. Within it are the flashed ruby on yellow pieces. The yellow bits within the blue are achieved by acid etching out the coat of blue.

At the bottom is Ros's signature - 'RG. 2000AD' - acided into blue glass, and the date the window was made. (Brain scans have the patient's name and date of scan on the bottom.) This signature includes Ros's trademark of a little crescent moon with a face.

"I love glass because of its magical quality. In the Middle Ages it was believed to have healing properties. I feel, after many years, that I am just beginning to understand its potential. I am particularly interested in the control of light through aciding, plating, staining and enamelling but am trying hard to simplify my work and concentrate less on the surface and more on the overall effect and the lead lines."

Ros Grimshaw

Day 5

BEHOLD IT WAS

Ros's description

The upper and inner right-hand light shows fish, fowl and sea monsters made more from my imagination than nature. Below I have shown the hope of a future with water for all taken from the depths of the Earth via the simple technology of a pump.

Main window

"Let the waters abound with living creatures.....and let birds fly above the earth"

At the very top is the Omega, from the statement that God is "Alpha and Omega". Beneath the colourful 'vault' (above the thumb line) and within God's thumb is a beautiful bird in Bariolé streaky glass. Below this a Concord bird in selenium yellow with various other flying fowls, including a flying duck above the pale brown cliffs that can be seen just above the spectacular Leviathan. The space between the birds is filled with opaque 'Wispy White' American glass with a slight streakiness in it.

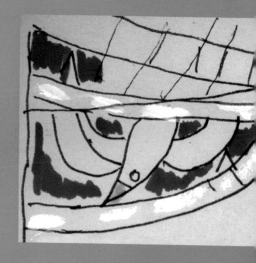

Day 5

And God said, "Let the waters swarm with the swarm of living creatures and let fowl fly over the earth across the vault of the heavens." And God created the great sea monsters and every living creature that crawls, which the water had swarmed forth of each kind, and the winged fowl of each kind, and God saw that it was good. And God blessed them, saying, "Be fruitful and multiply and fill the water in the seas and let the fowl multiply in the earth." And it was evening and it was morning, fifth day.

The Leviathan, or one of the 'Great Whales' that Genesis describes as a true monster of the deep, is made here in Hartley Woods' streaky-ruby glass. It has spectacular teeth made from prisms and it bathes in a sea of Hartley Woods' blue-white-streaky glass. Below the Leviathan are various other fish, one in gold-pink glass and a fine pair in multi-coloured streaky Bariolé glass hinting at the Pisces-pair so often portrayed in medieval glass for the astrological sign. The little pink fish with a blue eye is in glass from a box of gold pink glass from an old studio. Each of the fish has small round lenses or blobbies (see Glossary) for eyes!

In creating the various fish and birds here the glass itself very often suggested the outline shape: designing and cutting went hand in hand, the glass itself inspiring the creators.

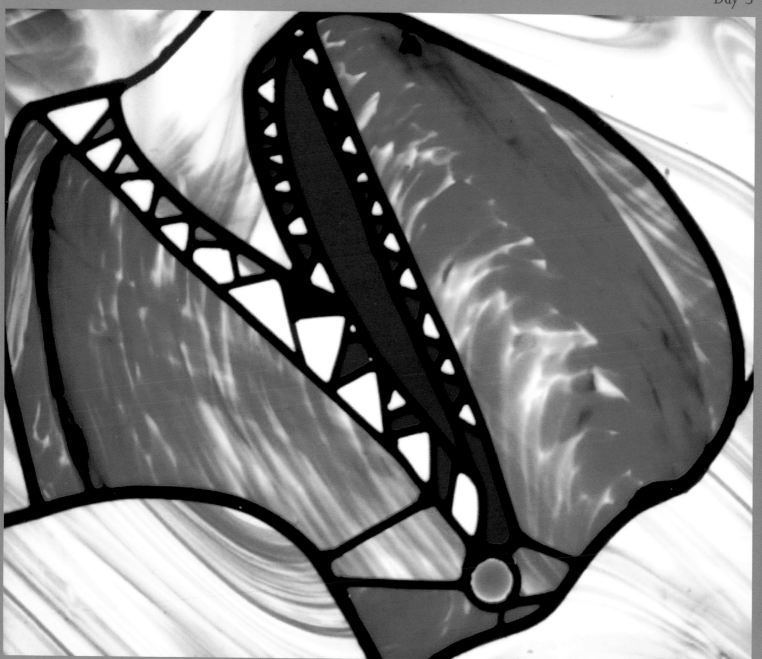

Patrick with a crystal tooth

Let the waters bring forth
that hath life and fowl that ma
And God created the great sea

Lower window
Water for everyone by using appropriate technology

The appropriate technology is symbolised by a pump rather than a dam. The pump is operated by a woman who is giving her child a good wash. It may however be her elder sister; this will have to remain as one of the window's unsolved mysteries! The pump and big sister's hair both use the brown glass that is also used for the two humans in Day 6. The orange/red/brown glass behind the pump is a favourite of Ros's which she calls 'Frank-Lloyd-Wright-walnut-veneer-with-a-hint-of-the-odour-of-sweet-sherry' glass! It is also used for the cow's head in Day 6. It is now unobtainable and was part of the suppliers' (Messrs. Creative Glass) 'Special Reserve', also known as 'The Lost Colour' since it was supposedly made "by accident many years ago" and the formula not noted down.

The girl's dress is made from the rich piece of old gold-pink glass that Ros also used in the flower in the lower panel of Day 3 and in the lower section of Day 1 – and in the tiny triangular pieces up in the traceries.

The child being washed is plated in sections onto a large piece of water-like glass called American 'Fracture and Streamers' - and this is placed on the outside so the figure is illuminated through the 'splashing water' just as if he was having his shower! The figure is a piece of 'graded brown' glass plated with white. Needless to say this was a complicated operation of plating and leaf-leading (see Glossary).

Day 6

VERY GOOD

Ros's description

The upper and outer right-hand light has humans, man and woman, cattle and creeping things with an African origin, the cradle of civilisation. The lower panel has an image of a foetal ultrasound, the double helix of DNA and the entwined snake symbol of medicine.

Main window

"And God said Let us make man in our own image...."

At the very top is a pink-faced angel with a nimbus-like crown, reminding us that Man is "a little lower than the angels" (Psalm 8). The dancing star is there perhaps to remind us of the birth of Christ as a man. The cow below is from a cave-painting containing the hand of a man receiving permission to create... Below the cow is a brown deer-like creature with long weaving antlers made in 'gratuitous' surface lead. Between this creature and the heads of the two humans is a horse-like creature. All these upper figures are inspired by early cave paintings.

This hand is in fact Ros's own hand and the design was made in the same way that it was, we believe, done 15,000 or so years ago: by blowing charcoal through a straw onto the back of the hand held in front of the paper – or cave wall as it would have been then. This was then engraved onto the red on yellow flashed French glass and took three days of careful steady work with an engraving tool.

Day 6

And God said, "Let the earth bring forth living creatures of each kind, cattle and crawling things and wild beasts of each kind." And so it was. And God made wild beasts of each kind and cattle of every kind and crawling things on the ground of each kind, and God saw that it was good.

And God said, "Let us make a human in our image, by our likeness, to hold sway over the fish of the sea and the fowl of the heavens and the cattle and the wild beasts and all the crawling things that crawl upon the earth."

And God created the human in his image, in the image of God He created him, male and female He created them.

And God blessed them, and God said to them, "Be fruitful and multiply and fill the earth and conquer it, and hold sway over the fish of the sea and the fowl of the heavens and every beast that crawls upon the earth." And God said, "Look, I have given you every seed-bearing plant on the face of all the earth and every tree that has fruit bearing seed, yours they will be for food. And to all the beasts of the earth and to all the fowl of the heavens and to all that crawls on the earth, which has the breath of life within it, the green plants for food." And so it was. And God saw all that He had done, and, look, it was very good. And it was evening and it was morning, the sixth day.

Below are two Africans, the 'humans' of Genesis. Note the little hearts as their eyes. Ros's models here were two of her friends who met at Windsor Terrace – and promptly fell in love! In the midst of this Love Story Ros designed the couple who discreetly hold hands behind the Kudu with his magnificent horns and blue side-burns. Note also their 'streaky' hairstyles and the 'blobbies' (see Glossary) that form their necklaces. The brown glass of their bodies is the same as that used for the woman operating the pump in the lower Day 5 panel.

The original design had one man here, but on reflection on the text – which described how on the sixth day God created "the human, male and female" – Ros was inspired to use a couple.

At the bottom is a Banyankoli cow from Uganda & Kenya with magnificent horns, emphasizing the importance of the domestication and companionship of animals with mankind. At the very bottom are the "creeping things".

The background of strong yellow is in fact selenium glass; Ros says she would not normally use it, but she needed a strong colour to off-set the powerful images and in this instance it works to great effect.

Lower window
Mankind in the future

The foetus was inspired by an ultrasound image, but uses a certain amount of artistic licence in that these colours were artificially added into the design. It employs beautiful streaky purple and streaky blue glass. Above, are two DNA spirals with the four acid bases A,C,T and D interpreted as blocks with the colours saffron, indigo, mint and madder. Beneath are two interweaving snakes, an ancient symbol of medicine and evocative of the cadeucis, symbol of the god Mercury, but also a symbol of the elements of life. Note the powerful projections onto the Refectory wall opposite.

There are three aspects to stained glass:
- firstly the fact that you can look through a piece of glass and see things the other side somewhat coloured and distorted.
- then there are the patterns of light and colour thrown onto the walls and floor of a building – or even onto the stone mullions that separate the main sections (or 'lights') of the window. This is wonderful at Chester, just after mid-day, particularly in the winter months when the sun is shining.
- thirdly, there is the surface of stained glass that can reflect light; this effect is exploited mostly with glass that is opaque or near-opaque to light and is most effective with glass that is iridescent, throwing many colours from the reflected light, regardless of whatever its own basic colour happens to be.
There is something very important in this three-fold aspect; all three are strongly present in the Chester window.

Ros Grimshaw

The love interest and the car chase

by

Rosalind Grimshaw

We know that no book is complete without a love interest and a car chase. About the time the window was being made at Chester, an old Ugandan friend, Charity, came to stay. I had met her through my Jewish friend, Angela, who met Charity when she joined a black woman's writing group. She was returning to Uganda after 38 years of working for the British Council. She had sold her house and was just staying here while she cleared up some last bits of business. We had been friends for a few years but our sons had known each other long before. They used to play basketball together and were both headed for art careers. Zac was a tall skinny thing with neat little dreadlocks, and my son Jem, was much the same only paler. Charity stayed for about three weeks and in that time Zac came to visit and realised this was Jem's house, which he'd always told his mother she would love.

At the same time (in another part of the forest) a chic New Yorker, Diana, who was destined to become another Eartha Kitt, had taken a room for the time she was studying at the Old Vic theatre school.

I was working on Day 6 of The Creation and, as those of you who have been paying attention know by now, God created man and woman in his own image and I chose to use Africans as the man

and woman for a number of reasons. Firstly, I wanted the whole window to move from Arctic night to hot African day. Secondly, I had always thought of Africa as the cradle of human existence. And thirdly, I had three beautiful models to base the figure of woman on, Diana, and both my sons' girlfriends. There was a great deal of discussion as the figure progressed of the true shape of an African bottom and other characteristics as she evolved steadily. We debated whether she would be innocent, or elegant. But we still needed a model for the man.

The day inevitably came when Zac came to tea. He was tall, broad, wore a suit and had lost all traces of boyishness – he was a big, strong man, working in the computer industry. Tea went very well, with many cakes – as usual – and eventually people arrived home from work and college. Diana came home and joined us and listened to Charity and Zac talking about their plans. I asked him if he had ever lived in Uganda, although it seems unlikely with his Bristol lilt, but he said yes, indeed he had, for a couple of years. His most vivid memory from this time was when, in a remote village, he had become very ill. He described how a distant uncle came to visit him and his voice came out of the darkness of the hut. He put his hand on Zac's shoulder and said in a slow, deep voice which contained the whole of Africa, "Son, do not be afraid."

In the long silence that followed, Zac's voice held like a magic spell in the room and all of us were enchanted. He and Diana disappeared for a few weeks after that – it was like a fairy tale; the Princess meeting her Prince. They were completely enraptured but, after a few months, they broke each other's hearts. But I had plenty of time to put them in the window.

About the car chase. I'm afraid you are going to have to find it in the window yourself. It is there, I promise.

"Get your saints dignified
and your faces beautiful;
show the majesty or the
sanctity you are aiming
at in these alone, and your
saint will be recognised as
saintly without his halo
of glory, and your angel as
angelic without his tongue
of flame."
Christopher Whall

21 March 2001

Dear Ros

I am so grateful for all that you did for Andrew and Steven and me today. It was lovely to be in your interesting home, and great to share in your studio. Thank you for your warm welcome and generous hospitality at luncheon, and for the excellent cuisine and wines! We much enjoyed the whole day, and being with Patrick, Carrie, David and Lavinia........

But today has, of course, been marked in a special and unforgettable way by seeing the Creation Window for the Chester Cathedral in the making. It was for me an historic moment, heralding the introduction into this community of a very beautiful, and sensitive and evocative work of art. Thank you for your special part in this inspired masterpiece, and for making it possible. I felt very moved and privileged to be associated in a minor way with what will obviously become a major creative enterprise.

So thank you all for a wonderful visit, and for everything you are doing so splendidly. We look forward to 4th July!

With very much love as ever,
Stephen

Letter

from
The Very Reverend
Dr Stephen S Smalley

Tradition

by Patrick Costeloe

27/6/02 – Painton is leaving after another session on the book. It is becoming clear that Painton is a considerably accomplished and skilled organist. On being asked about the organ tradition in France, and Paris in particular, Painton describes something that is common to the stained glass world.

Organists pass on their skill from generation to generation, from present to future. In Paris, going backwards, from present to past, the tradition still exists where many of the teachers studied with someone who studied with … someone who studied with … someone who studied with …… until one arrives at a composer, musician and teacher called Johann Sebastian Bach.

"Only connect", E.M. Forster's famous quote, comes to mind – though so true that it has become a cliché.

The connection here is that Rosalind Grimshaw was trained in a studio which was the second oldest in the country trading under its original Victorian name (J. Bell & Son founded in 1840), one of the oldest still trading, the oldest being Hardmans of Birmingham.

Joseph Bell passed the firm on to his son Frederick who then passed it on to his son Frederick, and the studio was in turn bought out and taken over by Arnold Robinson. Arnold Robinson, with his business and art partner, Edward Woore, trained with the 'Father' of the Arts & Crafts stained glass artists, namely, Christopher Whall.

Arnold Robinson's son, Geoffrey, who trained with Eddie Nuttgens – who in turn trained with Karl Parsons, another Christopher Whall pupil – took over the studio where Rosalind Grimshaw trained. The main influence on her artistic attitude to stained glass work is Christopher Whall.

Christopher Whall was not only an artist of considerable talent in his own right, but also a teacher of many aspiring stained glass artists through practice in his own studio and more widely through his book *Stained Glass Craft*. The most apposite quote applied to Christopher Whall's work comes from the American architect Ralph Adams Cram's response when looking at the Gloucester Cathedral Lady Chapel windows, that the windows are "at the same time perfectly medieval and perfectly modern".

The music playing on the CD in the studio is *Los Jovenes Flamencos*. The next generation of flamenco musicians (all from flamenco musician families) have learned, rejected, respected, rejected, remade and re-presented what will become a new layer in the history of the music. Tradition may not be alive and well, but it does seem, somehow, to be inevitable.

In the evening...

Concerning colour, Christopher Whall writes (in his book Stained Glass Craft printed in black and white):-

"... how hopeless to deal with it by way of words in a book where actual colour cannot be shown! Nevertheless let us try!
...... One thinks of morning and evening .... of clouds passing over the sun; of the dappled glow and glitter, and of faint flushes cast from the windows on the cathedral pavement; of pearly white, like the lining of a shell; of purple bloom and azure haze, and grass-green and golden spots, like the budding of the spring; of all the gaiety, the sparkle and the charm. And then, as if the evening were drawing on, comes over the memory the picture of those graver harmonies, in the full glow of red and blue, which go with the deep notes of the great organ, playing requiem or evening hymn. Of what use is it to speak of these things? The words fall upon the ear, but the eye is not filled.
All the stained glass gathers itself up into this one subject; the glory of the heavens is in it and the fullness of the earth, and we know that the showing forth of it cannot be in words."

The five main stages used to produce the panels for the Creation Window

Stage 1: coloured paper shapes are cut out and pinned onto a board.

Stage 2: when finalised, the pieces are glued down to form the collage.

Creating The Creation

APRIL 2000

It is early April 2000. Ros first hears about the Creation window through a call from the architect Andrew Arrol who asks her whether she might be interested in entering a competition for a new window in Chester Cathedral – and if she is could they please have a brochure by tomorrow!

By return of post Andrew receives the brochure and Ros and Patrick get the specification. What is needed is a large six-light window that has been something of a problem to certain other glaziers. The difficulty, apparently, is the even number of lights that make up the window: what can one do with six 'lights'? An odd number enables a symmetrical design to be considered around a central subject, but six? This is

no problem to Ros who with a characteristic flash of inspiration suggests:-

"The Six Days of the Creation."

Talking it through with her partner Patrick Costeloe, Ros is convinced that the idea of The Creation is absolutely right. They live and breathe The Creation for the ensuing weeks.

The specification requires that the chosen subject needs to accommodate aspects of the present and future as well as the past, in line with the Benedictine tradition of evolving Christianity in which Chester Cathedral has its origins. This, too, will be no problem for Ros since she has always seen the Creation as an 'on-going' phenomenon

Stage 3: full-size 'cutlines' are drawn on tracing paper.

Stage 4: using the cut lines as a guide, the chosen glass is cut to shape and laid out on a light box.

Stage 5: the glass is then leaded and cemented to form the final window.

that we witness in the daily evolving natural world – and the human species is a product of that evolution. The small 'lights' under the six main ones are ideal for containing 'modern' or 'updated' panels – one 'updated' idea for each Day of the Creation.

Genesis chapter 1 is read time and time again, initially in the King James version, then in some of the other translations and versions. The version by the Hebrew scholar Robert Alter particularly appeals to Ros. By the end of the week Ros, Patrick and her colleagues can almost recite the 31 verses by heart!

It is at about this time that Ros hears the Chief Rabbi, Dr. Jonathan Sacks, giving a talk at a

memorial service for Dr David Baum in Bristol. The theme of the service is:-

> *"And God saw everything that he had made*
> *and behold it was very good"*,

a passage that Ros instantly recognises as coming straight from chapter 1 of Genesis. It seems to be a signal to Ros that her decision to choose The Creation is the correct one. It is the words *"and behold it was very good"* that particularly stick in Ros's mind; they seem to infuse the whole story with a deeper meaning and sense of purpose that Ros needs to carry into her own creation. These words seem to be helping to solidify details of the intended design. She expresses her feelings at the time in a letter to Rabbi Jonathan Sacks:

An early sketch

"If the window wants a bit of any particular tint, put it there, meaning or no meaning. Put the colour in, anywhere and anyhow — in the background if need be — a sudden orange or ruby 'quarry', even a bit of a quarry, as if the thing were done in purest waywardness. 'You would like a bit there if there was an excuse for it?' Then there is an excuse: the best of all — that the eye demands it. Do it fearlessly."

Christopher Whall

"(The window was to be) the Six Days of Creation from Genesis chapter 1 and, below, man's continuation of the work. And running through the whole window the hand of God and a dove made from prisms … In my continual reading of Genesis I noted that God had made men and women in his own image as creators. It is man and woman's duty and pleasure to continue discovering hidden patterns, cures, secrets and harmonies in the universe. In the earliest cave paintings there are hand prints, some as stencils and others printed in patterns."

The cathedral authorities request a "little sketch" of what Ros has in mind for her initial submission — and they want it "by the end of June please" when the next stage of the decision process is due to be made. However, Ros replies that she "doesn't do little sketches", so together with Patrick and her assistant/PA Carrie Smith, they start the process of defining the detail for each of the six Days of Creation into a huge sketch some three feet by four feet.

MAY 2000

Early in May 2000, they pay a visit to Chester to check out the window and the Cathedral. It is to be in the Refectory, a long rectangular hall dating from the 15th century in which there are large windows at the east and west ends. The proposed Creation window is to be at the West end, facing the huge east window, filled nearly a hundred years ago with a rather unexciting design characteristic of its age with an overall grey-green hue and containing figures in typical "stained glass attitudes", as Gilbert and Sullivan once put it.

Ros and her party are spotted outside the Refectory taking measurements of the window, a somewhat unusual activity for potential burglars that soon gets the Neighbourhood Watch telephones buzzing. It is not long before their provocative activities attract the attention of the Estate Manager, Steve Nicholson, but he soon guesses who they might be and it is not too long before word has spread even further around the Cathedral Close. The Dean appears and introduces himself. This meeting begins an association which is to grow with warmth and respect on both sides over the ensuing months.

Returning to Bristol the studio plunges into what comes to be known as the "Mad month of May", the process of giving substance to the design, of filling in the subject matter of the Six Days of The Creation. With all the delving into magazines, books, photographs and the recesses of the memory, details gradually emerge: a river delta, stars, suns and moon, the Space Shuttle, fruit, plants, vegetables, a butterfly, birds, animals, seeds, fish, flowers, lightning, skyscrapers, flashlights and car lights, a brain scan, a foetus scan, hands and humans emerge. The vaults of Heaven and the dove of the Spirit join the soaring eagle and the Leviathan of the deep – all of these find their way out of the pages of the National Geographic magazine and other worthy publications and into The Creation – or at least into the sketch of The Creation as it is to be in the Chester Window.

In the meantime detailed measurements of the window arrive from Chester and a start is made on a life-size sketch of Day 1. This is initially carried out in pastels, but the process is clearly going to be impractical for the whole window: Ros's precious – and expensive – Russian pastels are disappearing faster than you can say "Refectory Window"! Thinking about colour and glass can induce strange things in the mind and it is at this point that the idea of doing the full size designs in paper collage – that could 'imitate' glass – dawns in Ros's mind.

…. and 'dawned' is the right word! Because of her Parkinson's disease Ros's day starts at about 5am when she has to organise her drugs. These mornings also offer the benefit of some peace and reflection before the activities and momentum of

the day take over:-

"The sun coming up every morning is like a daily promise of hope and the future", says Ros, adding *"even if it is hidden behind clouds and rain"*.

The growing light and the changing colours give her the idea of doing the designs in collage and of using only certain colours for the design of the window.

This is hard to believe when one is first confronted by the window in all its colourful finished glory, but this is perhaps the place to explain how Ros approaches colour in this window. It begins with a visit. Ros and her family spent the previous Christmas in Morocco, where she was fascinated by the colours used in the Imperial Palace: the four main 'Imperial' colours of saffron, indigo, mint and madder (red), as well as the bright red 'pepper' flower, the purple 'jasmine' and ochre. Ros discovered the powders for these colours (at a spice and pigment stall) in the main market in Marrakesh through whose narrow and bumpy streets Ros's son, Jem, together with Patrick, had negotiated the wheelchair. Viewing the pigments and revelling in their rich colours was like visiting Aladdin's cave. As they haggled over prices – an inescapable ritual in the conduct of any transaction in Morocco – another local tradesman tried to sell Jem a chameleon. This charming little beast obligingly changed colour whenever a new pigment was brought out of the box!

Having successfully negotiated a plentiful supply of various pigments and bought them back to England, Ros has been waiting for a suitable opportunity to use them – and the designs for the Chester window seem to be the ideal application. The colouring of glass is, of course, carried out by a completely different process (see page 109 and Glossary page 112) and it is the glass itself with its near infinite possibilities that will decide the final colouring. However, using the pigments to create a design made up of a mosaic of collage helps to weld together the spirit of particular colour combinations, and can only add to the inspiration of the final product.

JUNE 2000

As the day of the presentation to the Chester Cathedral authorities approaches, the 'sketch' begins to take shape. This now incorporates many pieces of collage displaying the Moroccan 'Imperial' colours. Defining the subject matter and carrying out the initial design fell into place during the 'mad' month of May, and now in June the final sketch is created by photo-reducing the large sketch, backing it with thin black paper and laminating the resulting window so that when it is held up against the light it gives some idea of what the final window will look like through transmitted light.

At the presentation on June 25th the design is received more enthusiastically than they can imagine. Indeed, the committee asks whether a full size design could be done before September. Ros and her companions are overjoyed at getting through the 'first round', only to be followed by the more sobering thought of wondering how they are to survive financially doing a full size design over the next few months. However, their fears are allayed; so enthusiastic is the committee about Ros and Patrick's proposal that they decide that the further stages of the competition do not need to be held. Understandably, an official decision and contract can not be given there and then, but the committee says that over the next few days it will seek to secure an agreement for a payment to cover their work to September by which time, it is hoped, the final decision will be made and the contract drawn up. The only reservation that the committee appears to have is whether the lettering of "AND GOD SAW" etc. will be legible from the ground. As it happens, Ros and Patrick have brought with them a leaded-up life-sized sample piece of the proposed window containing the lettering "AND GOD SAW ..... ". This is then placed in one of the lights in its anticipated final position for all to see and upon which to test their eyesight. No problems!

It is at one of these Chester visits that Ros discusses with Trevor Dennis important iconographic details, such as the authenticity of eagles in Genesis, as well as the nature of the Biblical Leviathan and the 'Great Whales' mentioned in Genesis. After much learned debate these details are agreed.

The submitted design

AUGUST 2000

Before going into hospital Ros prepares the raw material of the collage process by painting at Windsor Terrace numerous strips and sheets of paper with the Moroccan pigments. Each of these has to be hung up to dry all over the house, so that the place looks for a while like a Neapolitan backyard on washday. On August 16th she goes into hospital with her supply of painted paper, together with a number of pieces of soft-board and pins. Work begins by finishing the lower light of Day 1, begun at home, with its trails of car lights and skyscrapers. Cutting the strips for each trail is turning out to be a fiddly job: *"one of the most complicated things I have done in my life"* said Ros, since it essentially involves three colours which can often present problems to designers. Ros calls it a *"nightmare"*!

In the hospital the remaining five smaller panels are designed, roughly at the rate of one per week, by cutting up the appropriately coloured paper into the shapes of the coloured glass and pinning these onto the soft-board placed at the end of Ros's bed. A routine is established: when the final composition meets with Ros's approval the collage pieces are glued down and the design photographed. These are then hung around the ward for all to admire and to inspire the designers to yet greater things. It becomes clear part of the way through this design phase that supplies of painted collage paper are falling low, so sessions of painting paper are organised outside the ward – in the open air much to the surprise of other patients – where the sheets could dry more easily. Naples is once again seen, this time in Weston.

In early September Ros returns to Windsor Terrace: the hospital and its staff have got her onto a new regime and reasonably well stabilised. Work can now begin on the remaining five main lights. However, no sooner have they started than it becomes clear that the measurements they have

JULY 2000

In July the go-ahead is given to do the life-size designs and part of Day 1 is done in a few days at home in Windsor Terrace. But before the rest of the designs can be done some decisions need to be made about Ros's medical condition, the Parkinson's disease. Dr Bowman is *"the real hero of this story"*, says Ros. His declared main aim in life now is to get Ros from *"a gibbering wreck to a tax payer"*, as he puts it! To this end he has to get Ros 'off the pump' (injections) that have been her unpleasant life-line for the past few years or so. It is decided that August is the best time to do this, in order for Ros to be free to work on the glass selecting and cutting and the assembly phases of the project later in the year. This means a spell of some weeks in hospital right in the middle of the design period. However, this is not going to get in the way of things – and it is at this point that other heroes in the story come into the picture, namely the hospital staff at the Quantock Unit of Weston General Hospital.

Ros's hospital room

Dear Dr Bowman,

I want to thank you for coming to the dedication of the Chester window and for your letter. As people kept saying to me, "you must be so proud."

When I first heard of your Weston-Super-Mare clinic, I was at my lowest ebb. In September 1995 I had just come out of a number of weeks in a Bristol hospital where I had failed the 20-minute increased dosage of Pergolide administered by a junior doctor, who timed me running down the ward, cheered on by patients. By the time I reached the third dose I could not carry on or stop vomiting and was declared a hopeless case. I was offered the brain op. but apart from that was pretty much ignored, was immobile for up to 8 hours a day and frightened of everything. I had no carers, no benefits, no physical help and no hope - and no help from my G.P.

We met Joan Beer who told us the possible problems, but was positive and optimistic. When we met you, you described me as "unpredictably unpredictable" and then proceeded to admit me to your fine unit, where most of the staff had heard of Parkinson's disease. Then you started the long patient drug bargaining and balancing and the introduction of the difficult but miraculous apomorphine pump. You were unfailingly good humoured and always cheered me up and made me laugh, however bad I felt.

You built the drugs up slowly and thoughtfully, never changing more than one thing at a time: never giving credence to the possibility that I could not improve and become a sensitive achiever, and even a tax-payer again! The last five years you regularly and always listened to my complaints and adjusted my medication. Having built up my confidence and competence - and as I was beginning to occasionally turn green or abscess - you suggested I come into the rehab unit and exchange the pump for a combination of Pergolide and Cabergoline.

Having carried on with a regular number of small stained glass commissions, I was now involved with my first large cathedral commission, a 12 light west window, with a deadline of June 2001. My room in the hospital turned into a studio, where I carried out five full-sized collage cartoons for the lower windows in five weeks. I was given unlimited support by everyone, from consultant nurses, patients, specialists in specific information such as D.N.A., brain scans, foetal scans, etc. I felt like Lazarus (the Bristol glass maker).

I wish you all the best in your new career.

With many thanks and a big kiss
Rosalind Grimshaw

been working to for the sizes of the window openings are inaccurate. If ever Christopher Whall's quote of Turgenev, *"measure three times, cut once"* comes to mind, this is the moment. Clearly Patrick is going to have to go to Chester again – although not until the final go-ahead has been given and the inevitable adjustments can then be made to the already completed designs.

SEPTEMBER – NOVEMBER 2000

All through September, October and November the design process rolls forward, some 300 hours of designing and cutting up bits of coloured collage and gluing them onto the template. However, still no final decision on the window from the Fabric Committee of the Church of England. Nevertheless, appropriate glass is selected and reserved and instructions for the prisms to be used for the Hand of God and for the Dove are drawn up in readiness. Much of the glass is to come from Messrs. Creative Glass in Bristol combined with some pieces of 'old glass' bought in from the closing sale of the firm Hartley Wood. Some of this latter glass – for example, the 'Streaky Red' to be used for the Leviathan – is very old and may have been sitting on Hartley's racks for nearly 100 years!

There is much discussion now as to how to translate the colours envisaged in the design into glass: whether to search for appropriate glass or whether to plate two or more pieces together and to try to attain them. As so often happens in such things, the final decisions over this are made after the designs have been completed, i.e. at the moment of selecting and cutting glass coupled with last minute experimentation.

By the end of November the final life-sized designs have finally been completed. There is only one place that an image of such dimensions – 15 foot by 15 foot – can be photographed, and that is at the Spike Island Art Space (see photo opposite).

The workshop is ready to start cutting glass and actually making the window – but the Fabric Committee's decision is still anxiously awaited. To pass the time Ros starts making the two angels at the top of the two outermost lights. *"Well, if the project doesn't go through we can always use the angels somewhere else. There's always a market for angels"*, declares Ros philosophically, aching to get on with the window. And then, right on cue, the phone call from Chester comes, followed by the letter. It's all systems go! The Creation can now begin in earnest.

Ros and Patrick with the full size cartoon at Spike Island

DECEMBER 2000

On December 1st Ros and Patrick set to work, starting with Day 6. Throughout December, January and February they primarily work on Day 6 and on certain areas of Days 2 and 3. Although it might be thought tidy-minded to work methodically through from Day 1 to Day 6, in practice things don't always work out like that. Certain pieces of glass ordered from suppliers have not yet been delivered so certain areas have to be put to one side. Nevertheless, the delay and having to work without one specific piece of glass forces the glazier to think where else in the composition the same piece is being used: "I try to use the same glass to mean something different in each window, for example, a fish here and a planet there," says Ros. This means that during such a 'delay' a good visual memory is invaluable: it is like trying to hold a gigantic jig-saw puzzle in the mind. Fortunately this is no problem for Ros: "I have a good memory for a piece of glass – it can go across decades!"

Ros and Patrick decide at this point to create a chart for Dean Smalley so he can monitor the progress of the project. In fact the 'chart' is to be an illustration of the window onto which can be stuck photographs of the sections of the windows as and when they are completed. These can then be sent to Dean Smalley and his 'chart' gradually grow into full bloom as the months pass and the window emerges, somewhat like an Advent calendar.

JANUARY – FEBRUARY 2001

After Christmas in Tunisia, Ros and Patrick cut and lead Days 3 and 6 during January and February. The general programme of work involves Ros selecting and cutting the glass according to the cartoon but occasionally modifying it if a particular piece of glass suggests an alternative detail. The birds on the cliff in Day 5 were to arrive 'out of the blue' in this way. When the whole panel has been cut it is placed on a transparent tray and given to Patrick for leading.

A progress report is sent to Chester on February 15th in which Ros says:

"Some weeks ago I made a decision to avoid all painting in the windows. This was mainly for reasons of time and I decided to make the drawn line of the lead a positive asset. This has proven challenging in the use of glass and other innovative methods of glass treatment and has made the colour balance more crucial.

I have used a number of new techniques including engraving and complex plating as well as traditional aciding.

We are still waiting for the arrival of the 'Dichroic' lightning glass from the USA and some indigo from Germany. The prisms have been specially made and have arrived.

Apart from a lack of space everything seems to be progressing in an orderly fashion."

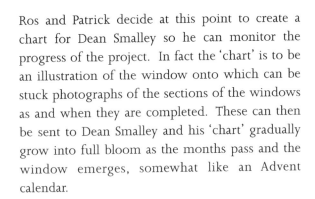

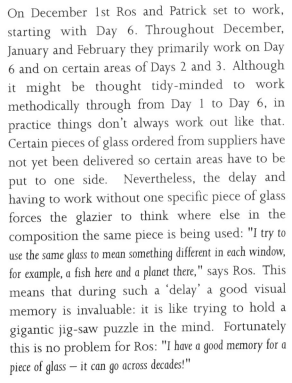

cutting the Leviathan
Day 5

MARCH 2001

March 3

Ros's birthday. Carrie, her assistant/PA, gives Ros a 'diary' or rather a sketch book that Ros decides to use as a diary of drawings. From her birthday onwards Ros keeps a record of what is done every day until the day when the windows leave Windsor Terrace for Chester Cathedral. Every morning, after her early rise, Ros draws in the diary what has been done on the previous day. Many of these are shown in this book. The diary actually starts on March 3rd, recording therefore what was done on March 2nd. That day includes cutting glass for the Leviathan (Day 5). Ideas are also entertained for the 'Hand of Man' in Day 6. This image is inspired by the hands that our primitive ancestors 'painted' onto the walls of caves such as Lascaux. In fact they are not painted, but portrayed by creating a 'shadow' of the hand by blowing charcoal and spit through a straw. Ros uses this technique, holding her own hand against a sheet of paper – just as they did in Lascaux some 15,000 or so years ago, holding their hands in front of the cave wall.

March 4 – 7

Choosing and cutting the glass for the cliffs and birds in Day 5 needs some last minute inspiration as bits of glass are seen already to 'contain' birds within them. Certain lines and colour shapes within the glass sometimes evoke birds in flight or standing on the shore. One cannot help thinking of Michelangelo 'seeing' the angel within the block of stone before he starts work. Some of these newly perceived birds are shortly to be released from their 'cages' in the glass into The Creation ....

The diary illustration gives an idea of what some of these bits look like after the lovely streaky glass had been cut and the birds 'released'. Visitors and bystanders comment that one of them looks a bit like Concorde – and is christened thus! Here again, the glass suggests the shape of the birds in the 'thumb of God' (Day 5). This time it is in lovely Bariolé glass. For some reason Ros says she has an image of Beachy Head and King Lear in her mind as she works on 'the cliffs' that house these birds: nothing too dramatic, we hope!

81

March 8 – 12

Work this week begins with the bottom panel of Day 4 – the brain scan with Ros's favourite pieces of glass. It is leaded up and photographed. More work is done on the thumb of God (Day 5): as well as on the Omega at the top of Day 5. The wing of the dove is started in this area: ultimately it will spread right across Days 2, 3, 4 and 5. It is made of clear 'quarries' each of which is a 'prism' with bevelled edges.

Meanwhile Patrick leads up the bottom panel of Day 5 – the child being washed under the pump. When it is finished the panel is hoisted up onto the easel and photographed.

March 13 – 14

Some reorganisation of the studio is required in order to facilitate a 'production line' arrangement so Ros's finished work can pass straight to Patrick for leading. A system is devised whereby glass, having been cut, is stacked in trays, with each 20-inch panel separated by a layer of paper. This enables Patrick to work methodically through each of the five or so panels that make each 'light'.

Day 5 is thus stacked into a tray, freeing Ros to start preparing the cutlines for Day 4. [A cutline, incidentally, is a tracing made of the cartoon (the design) showing all the shapes of the bits of glass, each being labelled with its intended colour. In this window the cut lines were made in 20-inch sections – each section representing a panel. These can be seen as the sequence of regularly spaced horizontal lines throughout the whole window: there are seven in the tallest lights and five or six in the others. The glass is then marked up for cutting against this series of 20-inch cutline charts.]

In preparing the cutlines for Day 4 special care has to be taken to ensure that the Hand of God, that extends across into the neighbouring Day 5, lines up exactly with where the Hand is going to be in the light next door, allowing for the thickness of the stone mullion between adjacent windows.

March 15

Ros continues choosing and cutting glass for the Cosmos in Day 4. The planet Earth is selected from a piece of glass that is nothing more than the bottom of a bottle – green and circular. Other planets are also selected from suitable glass pieces, or by 'plating', that is, combining two or more pieces of glass in layers.

It is time to start thinking about preparations for 'Dean Day', March 21st. Julie plans a big cake for Dean Smalley's visit to the studio. It will be decorated with a picture of the window.

March 16 – 17

Patrick's 'sigh' is presumably because of the exhausting leading-up involved in assembling the small lower panel of Day 1 – the skyscrapers with their little 'terrazzi' squares and the long trails of car lights made from long thin pieces of glass. Ros is quick to remind us that this small panel was exhausting to cut as well – a real challenge for everyone.

Ros is now well and truly 'in the stars', busy cutting glass and cut-lining the panels for Day 4 – The Cosmos. One superb piece of old glass that originally came from the Bristol Guild is intended to become a swirling galaxy, but 'explodes' into a 'super nova' of many pieces when attempts are made to cut it. This sometimes happens with glass that has been badly annealed. Nevertheless, all is not lost and some of the broken bits can be used.

The diary also notes that more work is needed on the cake for Dean Day.

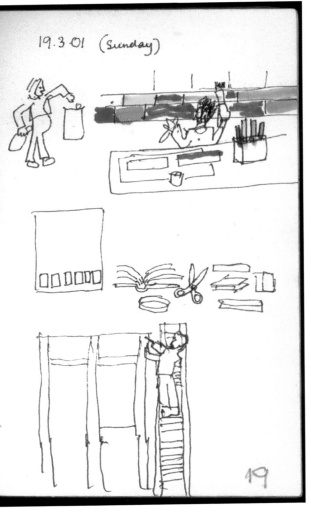

March 18 – 20

The leading of the 'lights and skyscraper' panel is at last complete. Patrick breathes a sigh of relief this time – rather than of exasperation. The panel is set up on the easel and photographed. Ros continues creating the Cosmos selecting glass for planets, moons, shooting stars – she's away!

The cryptic diary entry says "more cakes and more glass"! Clearly Dean Day is turning into a Feast Day. A pregnant Alice Ferguson is portrayed tidying up the studio in preparation for the visit. Patrick smartens up the easels with a lick of paint: these will display the complete panels for the Dean and his entourage to see. Ros works on the chart that contains the photographic record of the weekly progress on the window that is to be given to the Dean so he can monitor the project.

March 21

Dean Day finally arrives. Big sumptuous lunch. Enormous cake. Panels displayed, techniques and progress to date discussed. Lots of photos taken in the studio. (See Dean's letter, page 67).

BELOW: Carrie, Steve Nicholson, Ros, Dean Smalley, Lavinia, Andrew Arrol and Patrick

RIGHT: Dean Smalley, Steve Nicholson, Ros, Andrew Arrol and Patrick

March 22 – 26

Ros can be seen back at work again on the Cosmos after the festivities, working particularly on the great pale yellow sun with its rays at the base of the upper window of Day 4. Patrick is leading up Day 5 and it is finally put up on the easel for photographs.

March 27 – 31

Work on Day 4 continues. "Glass comes and glass goes" - a reference to an unfortunate incident when a beautiful piece of pink glass gets broken. By a piece of luck, at the same time, Patrick is in Bristol visiting the suppliers, Creative Glass, when he is told "*I have just the piece of glass for you*". He returns with a piece of streaky-pink only to find everyone looking miserable over the broken glass. "*Never mind – I've got some more,*" he announces to an astonished audience! Coincidence or divine providence?

Some exotic finishing touches are added to the sun in Day 4, plating its rays with some pale streaky red glass.

APRIL 2001

April 1 – 5

A bit of a break is needed and Jem's birthday celebrations provide a perfect distraction. Ros also buys her birthday books. Then it's back to work done on the top-most bit of Day 4. The diary says *"Carrie looking at 'Kane's Moon'"*; this refers to the moon at the top of Day 4, a half-crescent moon. The other half is inspired by a profile of Carrie's grandson. Ros also works on the 'fused angel', a figure just under the top line of the Hand of God next to 'Planet Bow Tie'. This is made up from a number of pieces of fused glass forming a pleasing jumble – amongst them a charming little face. This finishes Day 4 and, without delay, Ros begins drawing up the lead lines for Day 3. David Gilliland, invaluable throughout this project, photographs all the panels completed so far.

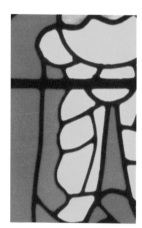

come straight from the garden and were eaten right after they had been portrayed. The whole experience of working on these seeds and fruit reminds Ros of the Garden of Eden that followed on from the Creation.

April 6 – 10

Day 3 well under way! In the illustration Ros and Patrick are measuring the angle of the line of the Hand of God, to check that the line follows across correctly from the neighbouring panels. Some changes are made to the composition of the forthcoming fruit and veg mélange that dominates Day 3. Photographs taken show the fruit, veg and flowers in various states of being cut and assembled. The bright red coloured pepper here – in fact a composition in two shades of red and one of yellow – is drawn and the selected glass cut in a matter of a few hours. The apples in the window

April 11 – 15

Ros can be seen in the sketch working on the blue background that lies behind all the fruit and leaves – apparently it is not easy to get a uniform quality of blue throughout the whole of this window – but she gets it right in the end. Carrie, Ros's assistant, designs the wheel-like orange at the top. Later Ros works on the big fig, its leaves and the melon. The splendid peas are modelled on products Esther has obtained from the market in Bath. Ros has fun cutting the glass for each of them – there are about 40! *"Thank goodness for the new oil-powered-Japanese-glass-cutter,"* notes Ros in the diary.

April 16 – 24

April 16th is Easter Day: Easter flowers, Easter lunch – and, of course, Easter eggs. The following day Carrie is cutting the orange she designed last week, while Ros presses on with Day 3. This is fast becoming the Longest Day – it seems to go on all week. One wonders if it was the same for the Almighty. By April 23rd, Day 3 is finally completed and photographed on the light table prior to despatching for leading. Patrick has just completed The Cosmos – Day 4 – and has put it up on the easel to be photographed. One slight hitch: Ros is not happy with the sun at the very top of Day 3 and decides it will have to be done again.

April 25 – 28

The new sun for Day 3 is rapidly completed and Ros begins work on Day 2 with the delta, sea and dry land. This is the most abstract of the windows with its expanses of interweaving channels in the river delta. There are some lovely colours here involving lots of 'plating': blue on purple, or blue on turquoise, or blue on streaky pink (see window description). The opaque grey glass of the shore alongside the delta is American. 'Quarries' are selected for the top of this window – for the Vaults of Heaven above the upper line of the Hand of God. One of them becomes known as the 'ghost quarry'. Another contains the 'Homage to Matisse' quarry, echoing the windows in the Rosary Chapel at St Paul de Vence, designed by Matisse in 1954.

On the 26th Ros and Patrick hold a seminar in the studio (Ros in her new shirt!) with a visiting class from the extra-mural Diploma in Architectural Conservation course Bristol University.

Chris and Kane install new racks for the growing number of completed panels. Cementing of the panels is mostly done under the gazebo outside – where the magnolia tree is in full bloom! Luke helps out here. (Cementing is the process of sealing all the joints between glass and lead to prevent water from getting in.)

MAY 2001

April 29 – May 3

Photographs are taken for the Dean's Progress Chart while more glass is cut for Day 2. May 1st is 'Happy birthday to the house Day'; it's 30 years since Ros moved in. She has had her stained glass studio here for six years. Cutting and plating glass for Day 2 takes up most of the time now. Luke is cementing completed panels outside. The diary notes "Need more purple". Much of this is required for plating with the turquoise glass for the river estuary. Patrick is seen bringing the required glass and lead back from Creative Glass.

A visit from Patrick's parents on the 3rd provides an excuse for a short break. They arrive as the two lower panels of Day 3 are put on the frame for photographing.

May 4 – 8

Ros and Carrie continue cutting glass. Day 2 is now nearly done and set out on the light table. Patrick continues working on leading-up Day 3 – apparently applying some gentle 'persuasion' with a hammer to fitting the orange into the composition. Luke is cementing out in the tabernacle in the garden. Ros's sketch shows that the magnolia is out – the year is moving forward fast – and, as the diary notes, there is only "1 month left…".

Friends Mary Gormally and Daniel Richardson visit on the 6th to inspect progress and Francis is the chef. On the 7th we read "*Andrea gets in on the act*": she is seen cutting glass with Ros in connection with the top of Day 2. Patrick is doing some clearing up – and, horror of horrors, he is smoking! This suggests a bad mood – possibly because there is less than one month left……?

On the 8th – Bank Holiday Monday for the rest of the world – we note that cutting for Day 2 has finished at last; it is now ready for leading. Patrick is portrayed wearing a new shirt – let's hope this improves his mood! Angela Baum's exhibition of elephant photographs is on at Spike Island, so everyone takes a break and goes to see it.

May 9 – 10

Day 3 is on the easel for photographing. Cut-lining of Day 1 begins – only one more 'Day' to create now…. A visit from clan Grimshaw (the Devon branch) prompts Patrick to get the swing chair out for them in the garden. Back in the studio it is business as usual – every day counts from now on. Ros is depicted awash with brown glass – a lot of it is needed for the forming earth on Day 1. Patrick is leading away, while Julie works on another of her excellent cakes, bringing cheer to everyone.

May 11 – 16

Ros has her eyes tested in the morning so she can replace the specs broken a few days earlier. Back in the studio she varnishes the eagle before 'aciding' with 'Brunswick Black'. The glass for the eagle is an old piece of Hartley Wood's brown on grey (flashed). This thick varnish protects the areas that are not to be eroded away by the acid to give a sort of 'kinetic effect'. Ros says "*I waited for a day when I had the 'wiggles', because I did not want an even surface!*".

The blaze of colour in the diary on 12th May is not a psychedelic doodle but rather an attempt at ideas for multi-coloured lightning using complementary colours – note the colour wheel – but in the end it was never used. The lightning in Day 1 was eventually achieved using thin pieces of blue glass that weave their way down from the dark blue Arctic night through the reds and browns of the forming Earth. Among these panels there is a piece of plated flashed red glass that looks like a swan, an effect produced by chance in the flashing process.

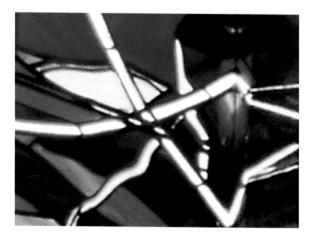

"*Not enough bevels*" says the diary: this refers to the long thin pieces of bevelled clear glass that make up the Hand of God. Some more immediately ordered! Patrick can be seen plodding around with lead and panels. The 13th is such a lovely day that a unanimous decision is made to have lunch in the garden.

May 17 – 19

Day 2 is up on the easel for its photo-call. Meanwhile the new bevels arrive – now God's Hand can be completed. A small accident in the studio results in the loss of some of the brown glass. Fortunately there is enough of the so-called "porridge glass" (or less politely known as the "vomit glass" in the studio!): this somewhat un-subtle 'sun-red' American glass is nevertheless ideal for parts of Day 1 where The Creator is trying to make sense of the Firmament .... trying to create Order from Chaos.

The top of the panel is reached: The Arctic Night takes shape. The star at the top – an image of a star-burst, possibly of the Big Bang itself? – has five points surrounding a round Swedish coaster all surrounded by iridescent pale blue glass. On May 19th Ros and Carrie celebrate their last day of glass cutting and Day 1 is now ready for leading.

May 20 – 23

Ros and Carrie start work on the collage panels for the exhibition that will tell the story of creating The Creation Window in a series of images to be on display at the cathedral – from the inspiration for subject matter, through design and creation, right up to installing the panels.

Ros spends the morning doing the accounts, ugh! After lunch she works on the small quarry that will contain the name of everyone who worked on the window or who helped in some way or other. The initial idea was to engrave this, but this was clearly going to take too long, so Ros decides to paint the initials onto the glass. This small piece of painted glass is then fired in order to stabilise it. The rest of the day is spent on the collage.

May 24 – 27

A period of tying up loose ends. Ros finishes doing the accounts – then returns to cutting up images for the collage. However the next day Patrick seems to be under a cloud: it looks as if he is doing his own accounts – enough to put anyone under a cloud. However, the good news is that Day 1 is finally up on the easel for its photographs. It is time to celebrate and Chris Beedell brings in the champagne, after which Ros is joined by Esther for more cutting up for the collage.

The streaky purple next to the eagle comes over nicely in the photograph – as does the blue

lightning. Looks as though someone (Patrick?!) has taken to the bottle (and cigarette!) amid the tension of the final days. Luke is still slogging away cementing and waterproofing the last panels.

JUNE 2001

May 28 – June 2

Patrick is seen doing some cementing – while Ros takes some well-earned time out in the garden; after all, it is Sunday. But soon she's back doing some manic collaging again – you just can't keep a good woman down. Some printing of text for the exhibition is done on the computer. Luke cementing some final panels while Patrick is up the ladder preparing for the next day's big photo-shoot.

The massive photo-shoot of everything goes well, but it means that Patrick gets plenty of exercise putting the heavy panels on and off the easel. Carrie's mum, Jean, pays a visit: she brings a beautiful orchid called – of all things – Angela Rippon!

Julie works on the Press Release. Luke fixes the car. Ros and David inspect the results of the photoshoot. Ros then continues with more collage... Patrick is doing some final leading. Janey Hall, the previous owner of the house, arrives amid the pandemonium to pay a visit and inspect all the goings-on. Collage can be seen all over the front hall area. Chaos reigns.

June 3 – 5

Jem and Frank film the collage and the panels before packing them into pre-formed racks for the car journey to Chester. Ros and Carrie are interviewed with Frank for the film. One final bit of collaging and then….. that's it!

On June 5th "*Post window depression*" sets in: Ros jots down her feelings:

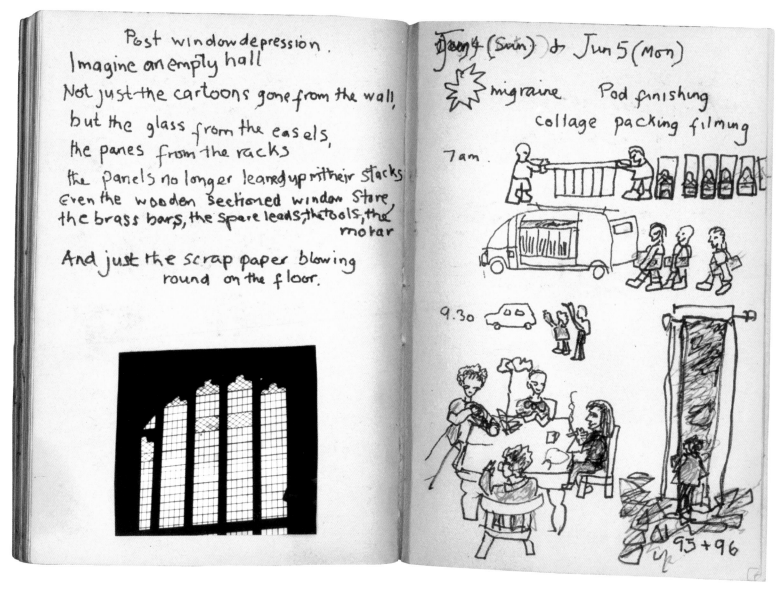

June 6 – 27
Patrick, Luke and Michael Lassen fit the window into the west wall of the Refectory. On the 27th everyone visits Chester to inspect The Creation in situ: it is a wonder to behold. A check that all is well – and, much to everyone's relief, it is!

Early July
One week's holiday in Devon.

July 26
Dedication of the window.

ABOVE: Ros and Carrie Smith supervise the installation

RIGHT: Hugh Brody, Ros, Debbie Cranston and Angela Baum

Ros and Dean Smalley with the Mayor of Chester and representatives from Chester College and The Royal Bank of Scotland who helped to fund the window.

Peindre d'abord une cage
avec une porte ouverte
peindre ensuite
quelque chose de joli
quelque chose de simple
quelque chose de beau
quelque chose d'utile
pour l'oiseau
placer ensuite la toile contre un arbre
dans un jardin
dans un bois
ou dans une forêt
se cacher derrière l'arbre
sans rien dire
sans bouger ...
Parfois l'oiseau arrive vite
mais il peut aussi bien mettre de longues années
avant de se décider
Ne pas se décourager
attendre
attendre s'il le faut pendant des années
la vitesse ou la lenteur de l'arrivée
de l'oiseau
n'ayant aucun rapport
avec la réussite du tableau
Quand l'oiseau arrive
s'il arrive
observer le plus profond silence
attendre que l'oiseau entre dans la cage
et quand il est entré
fermer doucement la porte
avec le pinceau puis
effacer un à un tous les barreaux
en ayant soin de ne toucher aucune des
plumes de l'oiseau
Faire ensuite le portrait de l'arbre
en choisissant la plus belle
de ses branches pour l'oiseau
peindre aussi le vert feuillage
et la fraîcheur du vent
la poussière du soleil
et le bruit des bêtes de l'herbe
dans la chaleur de l'été
et puis attendre que l'oiseau se décide à chanter
Si l'oiseau ne chante pas
c'est mauvais signe
signe que le tableau est mauvais
mais s'il chante c'est bon signe
signe que vous pouvez signer
Alors vous arrachez tout doucement
une des plume de l'oiseau
et vous écrivez votre nom dans un
coin de tableau.

First paint a cage
with an open door
then paint
something pretty
something simple
something noble
something useful
for the bird
place the canvas against a tree
in a garden
in a wood
or in a forest
hide yourself behind the tree
without saying anything
without fidgeting...
Sometimes the bird arrives quickly
but it could also take ages
before he decides
Do not be discouraged
wait
wait if necessary for some years
the speed or slowness of the arrival
of the bird
does not have any connection
with the success of the picture
When the bird arrives
if it arrives
observe the most profound silence
wait for the bird to enter the cage
and when it has entered
gently close the door
with the paintbrush
then rub out all the bars
being careful not to touch any of the
feathers of the bird
Then make a portrait of the tree
choosing the most beautiful
of its branches for the bird
paint also the green leaves
the freshness of the wind
the dust of the sun
and the noise of the cricket
in the heat of the summer
and then wait for the bird to sing
If the bird does not sing
It is a bad sign
a sign that the picture is bad
but if it sings it is a good sign
a sign that you can sign
Then you gently pluck
one of the feathers of the bird
and you can write your name in the
corner of the picture.

How to make a portrait of a bird

by Jacques Prévert

Dedication Day – the neighbour's story

by
Lavinia Ferguson

The window casts its many colours onto the wall of the Refectory during the Dedication party

On the day of the dedication I boarded the coach with a very excited party to go to Chester. There were many of Ros's old friends and neighbours, Janet and Marie, Jane, Debbie, Kate, my daughter Alice and her little baby Eva, and Chris from No 3 who, terminally ill and disabled, had organised the whole thing, the coach, the tickets, and even the refreshments, served by his grand-daughter Rose.

The day marked the end of an extraordinary year for me. As I pop into Ros's house nearly every day I saw the progress of the Creation Window from beginning to end. At the beginning it was just talking and thinking, dealing with a multitude of ideas and images gleaned from her childhood knowledge of the Bible and all that she has read and seen. Then a sketchy design emerged from which she built up the huge, multi-coloured collage that she used as a guide for the glass.

I would go in and find her surrounded by sheets of roughly painted paper, wonderfully coloured. The cutting out of shapes and sticking them onto the design. It looked haphazard to me, but when she pinned the sheets up and stood back it suddenly made sense and my faith was restored. It was during this stage that she went into hospital for six weeks. Far from being stopped her in her tracks, she just went on cutting and sticking and pinning up the finished sheets in her room. The bed and the floor were covered with bits of coloured paper, but the doctors and nurses seemed to enjoy their eccentric patient and kept looking in to see how she was getting on.

Then she was cutting the glass. Day after day she sat at her light table scoring and tapping and breaking the beautiful colours into jigsaw pieces. Carrie, her helper, was there assembling the pieces on the tray, juggling them around until they fitted together properly. Even at this stage the design was constantly changing. A new bird or a planet would suddenly appear out of the glass and had to be incorporated or an old piece of glass demanded a place. Whenever I went in Ros was working, often continuing to cut and tap while moving in an alarmingly out of control way. I would keep my distance and watch, trusting that there would be no damage. Amazingly, there was very little.

As each tray was finished it was passed to Patrick at the other end of the studio for leading. I never heard him complain though I think he must have, especially when Ros insisted that the strange shapes and tiny pieces were absolutely necessary. She kept experimenting with new ways of using glass. Nothing was impossible to her, so Patrick simply had to find a way too.

An exciting day for us all was the Dean's visit. A large proportion of the window was finished and the sections were hoisted up one by one for him to inspect. After the critical scrutiny and the erudite Biblical discussions we had a slap-up lunch in the kitchen and I went home merry and inspired. So, too, did the Dean and Architect.

The day finally came when Patrick and his team loaded all the sections into a van and drove them up to Chester. A few weeks later we were on the bus on Dedication Day. There was a great sense of fun – and anticipation, since none of us had seen the window in one piece. It was an exhausting journey for Chris, his last major outing, but he was determined to be there.

As the bus drew up outside the cathedral we saw Ros walking in, dressed in a long coat in dark red embroidered silk. The first part of the service took place in the choir and we sat at the side as observers. Then the great moment arrived when everyone walked through to the Refectory. The sun shone through the window spilling colours onto the walls and I wept. I looked at it up there in all its glory and felt very proud of Ros and so glad that I had been involved in a small way in this massive, vibrant and thoroughly idiosyncratic work of art.

Ros shares some thoughts

Over the months of putting this book together I have spent many hours with Ros deepening a friendship that began nearly thirty years ago. We have discussed, particularly, the making of the Chester window, but also her thoughts, feelings and insights on a whole spectrum of subjects. Living with Parkinson's disease has of course, been one of them.

Although not particularly 'religious' Ros does admit to feeling a kinship with the idea of the Biblical Creation, particularly the aspect that deals with Man's responsibility in his stewardship of the Earth and his relationships with his fellow Man. She says: "Man is the only creature that can now look after the earth and if we don't do this properly then we are not fulfilling our part." On re-reading Genesis, she identified strongly with the idea of the Spirit – the Spirit of God in Genesis that hovers over the waters of oblivion. It becomes the Spirit of the New Testament, available to help every man, woman and child whose soul is 'opened' to it.

"As a child I have vivid memories of pictures on the wall of my bedroom. One was of a farmyard and the other of a circus scene, both by the same artist. In both scenes the figures – animals, farmers and circus people – were portrayed in strong colours against a black background. I am sure this contributed in some way or other to my interest in stained glass and particularly to my love of using strong colours."

"What is so lovely about stained glass is that you make things – you don't put them together. I know it looks like putting pieces of glass together and holding the result up to the light, but actually during the making period each piece of glass becomes a point of focus. Then my own 'focus' - the imagination, or the creative spirit I suppose – adds something to it, perhaps another piece of glass alongside it or 'plated' to it and 'something new' emerges. I love not being in total control!"

"I felt this particularly strongly whilst making the Creation window….. this process of being an agent in the creation of something genuinely new and needed. Painton reminded me of the remark by the artist Paul Klee (whom we both admire greatly) that an artist is, in fact, 'a tool of the universe'."

Right from the beginning of my interest in stained glass I have been guided by the example and writings of Christopher Whall. He was born around 1850 and died in 1924. Through the Art Workers' Guild he met many of the leading lights in the Arts and Crafts movement in which William Morris played such an important part. What attracted me most about Christopher Whall's approach to making stained glass windows was its profound common sense and human-ness, if I might call it that. He had a 'family' like mine where relations, friends, hangers-on and apprentices all seemed to mill around on an equal footing –

and there were animals, birds in cages about the house. Yet making the windows was the number one serious business — and making them to the best of one's ability was absolutely vital. He was a great believer in perfection and would do all the necessary research in connection with a window before starting.

Unlike many of his Victorian colleagues, Whall believed that the glazier should be intimately involved with every stage of a stained glass window's production, from design through to final leading. Incidentally, I was sad that Patrick had to do the leading of the Chester window, but in the circumstances and under the time pressure we had no alternative. But Patrick and I had both been apprentices in the same firm — Joseph Bell & Son, where we met — and he had been 'in' on the window since its inception, so we were at least both on the same wavelength.

Whall's book "Stained Glass Work" has been my bible. I think it was the advice he gave on how to clean a 'badger brush' that first drew me to him, namely to do so "in the manner of an Italian waiter mixing hot chocolate"! Here indeed was a man after my own heart! He was full of sensible practical advice and particularly keen that his apprentices should develop their intuition. He once said something like: "if you think you want to use a particular colour — or piece of glass — do so, regardless of what others might think, or the prevailing 'taste' of the day." He coupled this with encouraging people to think in abstract terms and not just in terms of the pre-conceived composition — to allow whatever element that might appear by chance and 'seemed right' to prevail by modifying the original idea. Above all, he believed in letting the glass lead the glazier, rather than the reverse of imposing one's will onto the glass: if a piece of 'streaky' suggests a shape then work around that shape until it fits into your intended composition.

As an apprentice I worked in a stained glass studio — Joseph Bell & Son — where the proprietor, Geoffrey Robinson, had studied with a man with a direct link back to Christopher Whall. Very little was actually taught, virtually everything was imparted in silence by just working together at creating windows. It was a beautiful purpose-built studio at the top of the Bristol Guild, but freezing in winter and boiling in summer, with a wide and tall north-facing window — ideal for viewing one's work as it emerged. In these somewhat Dickensian surroundings that never saw the cleaner (glass seems to benefit from not being cleaned)

O how! Nay do but stand
Where you can lift your hand
Skywards: rich, rich it laps
Round the four finger-gaps.
Yet such a sapphire-shot
Charged, steeped sky will not
Stain light. Yea, mark you this:
It does no prejudice.
The glass-blue days are those
When every colour glows,
Each shape and shadow shows.
Blue be it: this blue heaven
The seven or seven times seven
Hued sunbeam will transmit
Perfect, not alter it.

"Mary Mother of Divine grace,
compared to the Air we breathe"
Gerald Manley Hopkins

we were referred to as 'the Loonies in the Loft' by the rest of the Guild! However, one thing I did learn verbally was how to cost a window — charge for everything, down to the last stick of solder, otherwise you would be out of business. When Joseph Bell did close down, Patrick and I were out on the street and we decided to set up shop at our home, where on the ground floor we have fourteen-foot ceilings.

"Since I have had Parkinson's I have spent all these years trying to get the message from the brain to the hand and one of the things that Henry (my brother, who sadly died very suddenly just before the Chester window project started) said was that

99

with Parkinson's things that are automatic in the body go on of their own accord, like breathing, heart-beating, digestion etc. The act of drawing, by contrast, is subject to the Parkinsonian movement. He pointed out that if I could make the drawing 'automatic' I should be able to create whether I was 'on' or 'off' (in the Parkinson's sense of whether I was being subjected to no movement, as sometimes happens). So I worked on that and carried on drawing even when the rest of me could not move, and that finally got the message through."

"The period of designing and making the Chester window has been a fantastically creative period for me. I think rather than calling the drawing 'automatic' I mean being receptive and 'seeing' things and looking at things without any intellectual analysing and just letting the drawing 'happen' of its own accord, as it were."

"It has not been easy, of course. Just after I obtained the commission to do the window my consultant suggested that before I get too deeply involved, he get me off the Apomorphine infusions for the Parkinson's and onto a complex regime of drugs that includes Cabergoline. So I had to spend a month or so in hospital whilst they monitored the change over. This now enables me to work up to five hours a day which is a great improvement – and, of course, it is a relief to be off the pump!"

"I have given up so many things in my life now. I hardly ever go out and my life has become so much simpler and more focussed. So much of what went on during the making of this window was simply fantastic! All sorts of things and oddities, such as what I was reading, the people I met, what I heard on the radio or saw on television – a whole spectrum of things just 'happened' and came about exactly when they were needed."

"The window is about the Creation, about Nature, so my own garden is particularly important to me. It helps to weld together the overall feeling of the partnership of the Creation Window with Nature, light, the seasons, trees.... with my own life and the evolving times in which we live. There is a plant in the garden, a quince Japonica, that has red flowers in the spring and in the autumn makes the dullest sludge-coloured apples. But when they are cooked they make a pure pink jelly. I see this as a kind of alchemy, just as stained glass work is a kind of alchemy. Sand and ash are turned into this fantastic substance, glass, that can play with light and colour. Human input then arranges the glass, then Nature takes over and the ever-changing light displays its magic to us. It is a kind of visual pure gold. Before stained glass came of age, almost a thousand years ago, the Byzantine world represented the Divine 'light' that pervaded holy personages by the colour gold that often surrounded them: gold mosaic in the churches, and gold leaf in the icons and paintings. With stained glass, the light can itself symbolise this 'Divine Light' pervading every piece of glass, changing itself with infinite variety as it passes through. In the churches and cathedrals it illuminates stained glass personages, patterns and scenes, while inviting the beholder to share in this element of the Divine ..."

"A particularly magical thing about glass is this way that it changes with light. At different times of the day, or at different times of the year, or in different weather, different pieces of glass in a window come to life...... as if each piece has its own particular time and moment."

"This is the way in which the window is linked to the natural world — to the Creation as it evolves through our times in what we call evolution. There are some trees outside the Refectory at Chester that cast their shadows onto the Creation Window, moving in the wind, coming and going as the sun moves in and out of the clouds in a kind of Divine Symphony."

"Painton mentioned to me that there was a belief in medieval times that making stained glass involved using jewels. Since light reflected off jewels was believed to have the power to heal people then stained glass windows, that imitated jewels, hinted at this power. I took this idea with a pinch of salt, as do most people, although I believe that gold dust has been used for making certain red glasses for many centuries, although not, we are told, in medieval times. But Painton also suggested that certain stained glass windows seemed to him to have a kind of 'power', even though they were certainly not made from jewels. He suggested that it was not just being in the presence of these windows that brought about the healing but being involved with them that also worked their 'power'. In photographing and researching his own 'Rose Windows' book a kind of miracle was being wrought within him.

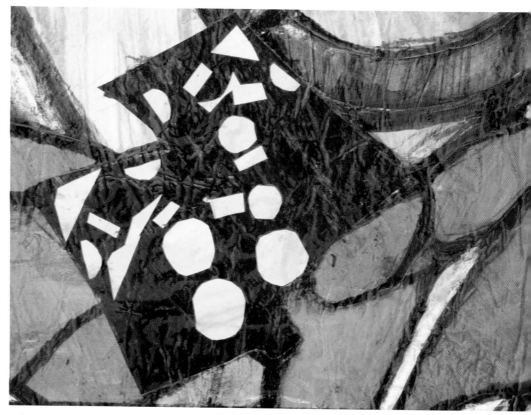

In my own life I feel that making this window has brought about amazing changes in me that amount to a kind of healing. As Rodin once said concerning medieval art:-

'In the calm exile of work we first learn patience,
    which in turn teaches energy, and energy gives
    us eternal youth made of self-collectedness and
    enthusiasm. From such vantage we can see and
        understand life, this delicious life that we
    denature by the artifices of our enclosed, unaired
    spirit, surrounded though we are by masterpieces
            of nature and art.'

Matisse in his advanced years took to collage, often working from his wheel chair — and I feel a kind of empathy with that in doing this Chester window. Matisse's own interest in stained glass came later in his life, and the chapel at Vence in the south of France was designed by him as a kind of 'thank you' to the nuns of the Rosary who looked after him when he was ill.

I feel a strong link with him in this connection. But it is also his interest in collage, in areas of colour and simplicity of line that I share. Painting paper and then cutting it into shape is just like cutting glass — in the designing sense — and much more satisfactory because one can 'see' the window before it is actually made.

I am fond of the poetry of Gerald Manley Hopkins, particularly those lines from "Blessed Virgin Compared to the Air we Breathe":-

'The glass-blue days are those where
        every colour glows...'

and, of course:-

'The world is charged with the grandure
        of God...'

I hoped I have managed to infuse something of this spirit into the Creation Window.

Parkinson's disease

The following is a letter from Ros's consultant at Weston-super-Mare Hospital, Dr C.E. Bowman, to Mary Baker, then Chief Executive of the Parkinson's Disease Society, dated 5 February 2001. (See page 120 for PDS contact details.)

Dear Mary,

I think I have told you of Ros, one of my Parkinsonian patients. She has had huge problems with Parkinson's disease which with my little bit of knowledge and a great deal of luck and Ros's resolve, we have to an extent overcome. Ros is an internationally renowned stained glass artist and before we made progress with her disease had been unable to work. She is now able to work and competed for and won a commission for a very large window in the Refectory of Chester Cathedral. Indeed she was doing some of the work for this in terms of planning whilst on an extended in-patient re-assessment of her disease towards the end of last year. My understanding is that the window, the glass of which has now been cut, is due to be unveiled in the summer.

I think it would be a fantastic opportunity for the Parkinson's Disease Society to get involved with this in some way. I enclose a photocopy of what the window will be like and should add that it is some 30 feet high in reality and you will see in the fourth panel on the bottom there is a scan of Ros's brain indicating her Parkinson's disease. In the picture you will also see the outline of the Hand of God. I have to say the window will be far more spectacular than this picture can do justice. It has been enormously exciting, and encouraging, for the staff at Weston to be involved with this project and I think that such positivity is something that many other people could benefit from.
My kind regards

CE Bowman, Consultant Physician

Ros's connection with the Parkinson's Disease Society has been through several small incidents.......

1. When I was finally diagnosed I was put into contact with the local Branch Officer who came to see me quite soon. I succeeded in dropping a tray of tea, china, cakes, sugar and milk all over him as we went up the stairs. I have not seen him again!

2. We did once go to a local meeting – just to see. When we got there we were so alarmed by the wiggly wobbly people and the frozen finger food that we swapped identity badges, played a bit longer and then went to the local supermarket – where we saw even more wiggly wobbly people!

3. We became really desperate when I became immobile for up to 8 hours a day. My consultant took me into hospital and started testing a new drug on me. He made me run up and down the hospital ward with increasing doses until I was so sick I stopped. All the punters were very disappointed. My daughter Esther and a friend sprung me later that night.

I thought perhaps there might be some better treatment available and consulted the PDS Head Office. Their geographic knowledge outside London was a little sketchy, but the Salisbury PDS Nurse agreed to come and visit me in Bristol on her way to Cornwall for her summer holidays. She then had a brainwave – wasn't Weston-Super-Mare somewhere near Bristol? We went straight there and discovered 'Parkinson's Paradise' - a full time PDS Nurse (Joan Beer) and other associated workers and a consultant from heaven (CE Bowman) who took me in, sorted me out over the next six years and used my case as the subject of his lecture on the occasion of Mary Baker leaving the Society.

There is still no PDS Nurse in Bristol but I can't speak too highly of the Weston-Super-Mare team, who allowed me to use their unit as a studio for 6 weeks.

I should like to mention the Society's excellent scientific research projects. I myself was involved in a fascinating project in which I was injected with radiation and people in a simulated spaceship watched me – twice.

Able in my dreams

by Patrick Costeloe

"I am on a beach. It is a glorious summer's day. The smooth sand glimmers, golden ridges shaded with the wave shadows of the retreating tide. And I am running along the water's edge, splashing drops of sea water, pearls of it on my legs, jewels of it glittering in front of my eyes... and I am running... running... running..."

Rosalind's dream.

We have been on three research programmes, have looked at alternative therapies, have experimented with different drug régimes, have read anything and everything comprehensible to us on the subject of Parkinsonism and neurology. We have recently been introduced to the idea of surgery, namely pallidotomy, and are see-sawing between this surgical option and going for a pharmacological option in the form of Apomorphine injections. One of the neurosurgeons pioneering the pallidotomy came out with a very reasonable justification for it: "When L-Dopa was discovered as a treatment people were given the choice of an operation or a tablet. It's obvious which course of action they wanted to take." However my partner is now faced with a choice of an operation or a needle: not quite such an easy choice. It has been thirteen years now that we have lived with this unpredictable and bewildering condition called Parkinson's disease.

103

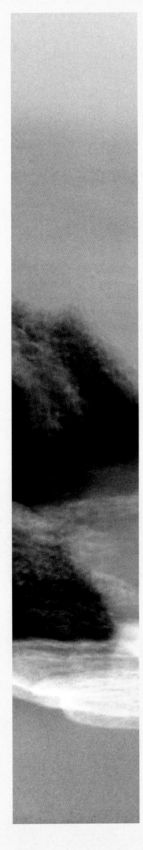

I am a 'carer', something I had not thought of myself as for the first ten years of my partner's Parkinsonism. Carer! A word so hated by so many. But it has meaning to any man or woman with a deep or intimate relationship with any other man or woman without regard of – ability or disability, but love, and love only. Why did it take so long for my status to become clear and have a name? Simply because my partner refused to think of herself as a 'caree'. I apologise for the word 'caree' because I am not sure that it is a real word; but the word 'patient' is so inappropriate to my impatient partner and the word 'sufferer', though true, just rubs salt into a hopeless wound when we are trying to find hope.

The state of 'denial' has acted as an extraordinary experience, sharpened by the fact that we are a creative unit. Rosalind, my 'caree', is a stained glass artist and I am a writer so we have had the added dimension of experiencing and expressing Parkinson's through the crafting of colours, forms and words.

My "practical project or proposed initiative to improve the quality of life of people with Parkinson's disease and/or their carers" is, on the face of it, very simple and is not my idea, but my partner's. It is a suggestion she made to somebody researching Parkinson's disease. If I remember rightly – my memory is terrible in comparison to hers – she had just done a series of tests for a psychological research team. These tests (number, word and memory) would have completely floored me, but to her they were easy. On the face of it I was the one who was impaired. She felt that everybody working in the field should spend at least a whole day with somebody with Parkinson's disease.

This seemingly very simple, practical idea I want to combine with my experience of many years as the partner of somebody with Parkinson's disease. Given that Ros was diagnosed with a condition usually associated with old age at the tender age of 37, the progress of the condition has inevitably cut right across our working life.

My account of this experience is an attempt to put the reader of this essay right into the heart of Parkinsonism, and Parkinsonism as experienced by a carer. The metaphor running through this essay is that of a traveller in the 'Land of Dis-ease'. Understanding and accepting this 'Land of Dis-ease' leads to being a native of a 'New World' every bit as legitimate as 'The Normal World'.

Come to think of it, the idea of a traveller in the 'Land of Dis-ease' is not a true description. The word 'traveller' gives the idea of choice – as though the right equipment has been bought, route maps and guide books perused and the right currency changed.

Travel is too active a word, as though we were the initiators of this journey. I know I did not chose mine and blame my partner. But that is not fair either. She didn't have any choice and I think it would be better to describe her as the 'initiated into this journey'. She has become an unwilling native of this unpredictable 'New World', just as I have become an unwilling witness of it.

The predicament of the witness is more like that of a traveller than a native. There are times when I feel as though I have tagged along for the ride, on the journey neither of us wanted. It is as if some sadist has dumped us in the middle of nowhere and told us to get home. We have been left without a compass, matches or even walking boots. Even worse, Ros moves when she doesn't want to and cannot move when she wants to. This means that not only are we making the journey home very slowly but she is demoralised by despair and depression. This in turn makes the surroundings seem all the more bewildering and terrifying. Control on this expedition seems irrevocably lost.

On top of this, the outside world seems to be getting more confusing. The experts on this kind of journey are observers. They are one more step removed from 'The New World' than carers. Carers are stumbling along with the carees. And the experts are watching the carers and carees stumbling along and giving opinions and encouragement based on their study of the detailed maps which describe the landscape, and knowledge gleaned by their experience of watching a number of individuals attempt to come to terms with their surrounding landscape.

The experts are cartographers of the condition but are in danger of confusing parts of the maps as being representative of the whole landscape. Details such as forest and hill do not show the trees blown down in the high winds of March, the gorse and heather that flash gold and purple as the clouds scud across the sky and the sun bursts through. A map is a series of markings and is not to be confused with 'the thing in itself – 'der ding an sicht'.

The cartographers compete, and in so doing are in danger of losing sight of the landscape! Of the three research programmes we have been involved with one was involved with Parkinson's and perception (especially in artists), one with Parkinson's and psychology and one with Parkinson's and neuro-chemistry. The psychologists and neuro-chemists seem to be at loggerheads and the neuro-chemists seem to be at loggerheads with each other.

All these 'cartographers' I have met are perfectly charming on a personal level. It is the 'cast of mind' running deeply through the research establishment that I question. As the areas of research become more and more rarefied there is a danger that the very real sufferings get lost in the science. Medicine is losing the sense of the whole person; I know this to be true in my partner's case because this plea I have heard for years and years. As bio-neuro-chemist-psycho-surgeonologists struggle through research and experiment so the rocket of knowledge seems to have lost sight of the travellers on the ground.

I have turned back many times to Oliver Sacks' book *Awakenings* because his patients are treated with a rare humanity, respect and imagination – an imagination so far reaching and sensitive when confronted with such a painful, paradoxical and devastating state of affairs that it turns to metaphysical poetry for illumination. It is not that Sacks is necessarily right, but the qualities he brings to bear in writing about Parkinsonism cannot be wrong. It is this strange paradox: on the one hand the sophisticated developments in the knowledge of biochemistry of the brain or pharmacology; on the other the despairing (almost suicidal) heap of human being, statuesque in stillness but as perceptive and sensitive as the decade before diagnosis.

In saying this I am aware of being in danger of biting the hand that feeds, of doing down the experts, the organisations and helping hands that are God-sends in this sorry journey. The travellers, by this I mean the carers and carees, are in a very vulnerable position. We may hold opinions we are afraid to express in case we alienate those we need to help us. The environment of those who help and research can never be the same as that in which we find ourselves.

For example, the six-monthly consultation with a specialist only gives a half-hour insight into what has been some one hundred and eighty days of struggle just to keep going. Of course we would like to be airlifted immediately out of 'The Land of Dis-Ease'. But we know that at best we'll get an adjustment to the tablet regime which will flatten out the gradients of the steepest hills and make the rivers flow a little bit more slowly. In other words, make the landscape a bit easier to be in and live with. I do know that all those involved in the research, help and care would also like us airlifted out.

My criticism is based on an opinion of the environment that the 'Old World' we once inhabited seems to be like. The statuesque heap in the corner of the consulting room is, in my case, the same heap that has watched as an exhibition of her work, a one-man show, has been hung in a prestigious London gallery. Oh paradox of paradoxes. And, to make us an even more difficult pair of cusses, we have existed for years in that wonderful state known to psychologists as 'denial'.

The confusion caused by 'denial' is total. Firstly, the carer is in the precarious position of going along with it because for 'denial' to be effective it requires absolute belief and collusion. This leaves the carer liable to accusations of not caring when situations crop up that are undeniable, like inability to move when some movement has to be undertaken. This is even more acute, obvious and, at times, 'undeniable' for the caree. As for the visit to the specialist, let me just say that in my experience our two-person orienteering team has suffered badly from my partner's inability to suffer in front of the consultants.

On the contrary: she pulls herself up to her full height, the dyskinesia settles down, her rigidity is crushed by a fluidity born of pride and will, and as for being disarthric, well, words once swallowed are rolled on the tongue like sweeties. Since four in the morning (insomnia is an added bonus in this land), she has been worrying about adjusting her habitual drug régime for the sake of getting to the consultant, about what to wear, about whether we will get there on time (even though we'll wait for hours when we get there). All this anxiety, bad enough in itself, only serves to set off a stream of Parkinsonian symptoms which have to be overcome before we get to see the consultant or else he won't think she is very well!

This feature of our bizarre landscape I will call the precipice of paradox and it is one we will both have to learn to love because it crops up constantly. In fact it is a feature so constant that it is almost like a background or contour line that describes the rise and fall of the landscape.

So we present ourselves to the consultant. If she's going to deny she's ill, there's no way I'm not going along with it. It has been a strategy for survival for so long that I'm not going to pipe up that things are not so good. And so the poor old consultant has to analyse and adjudicate on a false premise.

"You're doing well ... How long have you been diagnosed now? Two... four... seven years ...And the prognosis?... Is good. Here is a traveller in 'The Land of Dis-Ease' who's traversing the terrain much better than one would have expected." The Consultant can't say "I'm surprised, you shouldn't be doing this well. The prognosis isn't too good."

So here we are, pretending it isn't that bad and is there any way that she can be tested, like a scan? No way, too expensive on a casual basis. As it happens the only scan, the MRI (we've been there on one of the research projects), is mainly used, at the moment, to test people who might be faking Parkinson's. Talk about the precipice of paradox: there are people who would pretend to be in this 'Land of Dis-Ease' just as we pretend we're not in it!

The more I use the metaphor of travelling in a strange land to try and illuminate the predicament posed by Parkinson's disease the more apt it seems. One's landscape, one's environment, is so much part of one it is like breathing: miraculous, but taken for granted. A concrete example of this is the stained glass studio where my caree and I worked for many years. The work is wonderful in every way: from the materials, particularly the coloured glass, to the rhythm of the stained glass craft which is almost as labour intensive now as it was in the Middle Ages. As for the studio itself, it was as magical as the craft practised in it. Old and Dickensian in some ways, but steeped in the Arts and Crafts tradition with fragments of old stained glass panels, framed drawings and designs, a stone carved by Eric Gill as a sample for a tombstone, etc. All this we took for granted until it was closed down very suddenly. And suddenly all the objects that were just part of our environment became something different. Our whole environment collapsed, breathing became difficult and we wondered what on earth to do. There was only one way forward: to build our own studio. And we did it. And now it is up and running it is just as wonderful as the old one. We can breathe again. This example, traumatic as it seemed at the time, is so minor in comparison to the process of adjustment provoked by the diagnosis of Parkinson's disease, but it is the closest I have come to having one world collapse and having to create another one.

There are times when I would not wish it on my worst enemy to spend a day with someone with Parkinson's disease. Needless to say, all those involved with research and treatment, the Parkinson's Disease Society and others, are lifelines, faint flashes of hope in the dark.

"I wake up. It's dark and cold and I can't move, can't even turn over. I try to go back to my dream. I was running by the edge of the sea, just running and running and… but I just can't get the dream back. It's gone and I can't get it back. Pass me an extra half tablet will you. I'm stuck. Have been the last two hours. But it's strange isn't it. I was able in my dreams." Rosalind wakes up.

The glass is taken from the furnace — a glowing blob on the end of a long metal tube — then blown into a bubble, swung from side to side, spun and rolled on the bench. Each man has a thick pad like a falconer's gauntlet on his forearm. The blob of glass is passed like a baton from one man to the next, turning from blob to bubble, bubble to balloon, balloon to muff. Everything is done with enormous skill and ritual, the men working for four hours non-stop, dodging and weaving, blowing and rolling — and always in silence.

Each day is one colour, yesterday was blue and today white. The muffs or cylinders are wrapped in cardboard coats to protect them while they are cooling, and before they have become cold they are scored with a glass cutter. The next process is the flattening and annealing.

The next day they are lined up on a conveyor belt (the modern technology) and move slowly towards a fiery furnace. Here, in a bed of flames, the muff is eased open along the scored line and gradually, carefully flattened. At this stage it looks nearly liquid and has the strange illusion of water in a flame. The craftsman eases it flat with a kind of croquet hammer made of poplar wood which as soon as it touches the glass catches fire and burns and chars as it flattens the glass. At each stage the furnace is closed for a moment. The flattened sheet of glass travels back slowly on the conveyor belt and at the end of the line, for some reason to do with exporting to America, the soft

Visit to Hartley-Wood Portobello Glassworks Sunderland

by Rosalind Grimshaw

November 22nd 1988

There was snow on the ground and slush in the streets and the glass works was the first warm place in days.

The most striking initial impression of the glass works was that no one spoke. I was led past the furnaces to where the team of four men were performing their slow and skillful dance of glass-blowing.

flowing edges of the glass were cut off and the uniformly sized rectangles were stacked ready for packing.

I asked if I could see the chemicals used to colour the glass; I was tentative as I know this is perhaps the most secret part of the whole process. I was taken into the back of the yard to an old storeroom full of polythene sacks and large bins with shovels deep in a white powder not unlike French chalk. The secret was as old as alchemy – the fire turns this dirty powder into pure sparkling coloured light.

After watching the making for some time I was finally led into the treasure house where rack upon rack of coloured glass is stored. I could chose what I liked – and I wanted everything! Each sheet is unique in texture and colour. It is the imperfections that give the glass its quality, the ripples distortions and bubbles which break the light; even bits of dust add interest and quality.

I had naively hoped actually to blow some glass and even colour some but it was obvious from the moment I arrived that this was out of the question. The whole place was almost masonic in its silence and lack of verbal communication. The trust, intimacy and understanding between the men and the ritual passing of molten glass was identical to that I had seen in Murano, Mallorca and Barcelona. It was obviously built up over years and would have taken considerable skill and time to infiltrate. Even the men in the office were not going to talk and the only women were firmly behind typewriters or making tea.

I chose my glass, paid for it and saw it packed, then boarded the train back to Newcastle and south to York. The snow sparkled and the winter sun set, changing the sky through every glass colour – ending with a triumphal, exotic streaky gold-pink on blue.

109

Some examples of Ros Grimshaw's other work

Fan Light. This is a tree outside Ros's house at Windsor Terrace. It is portrayed at differing times of the days and of the year.

'Rosalind' as in 'As You Like It' (private collection).

This fairy is to be found in a grotto in Windsor Terrace. She is based on Marilyn Monroe and portrayed amid clematis, roses and Lady Fritillary.

Pan in the grotto, although on a different wall and with different light. The model this time is Patrick Costeloe.

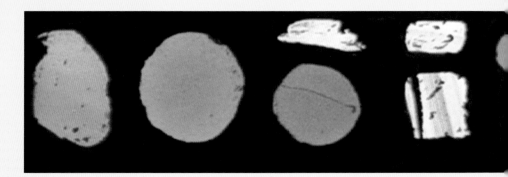

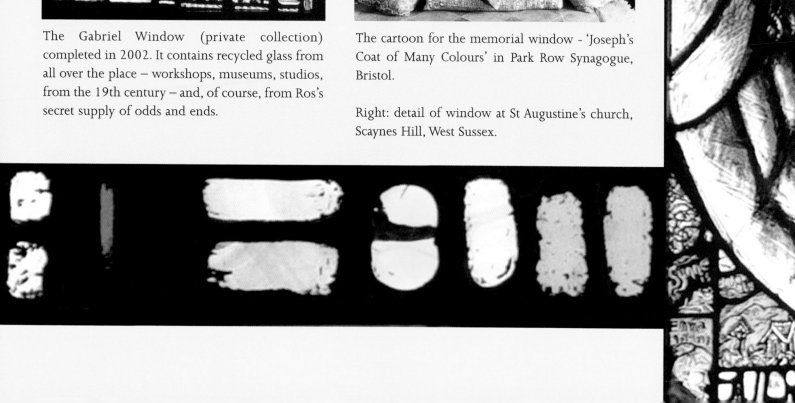

The Gabriel Window (private collection) completed in 2002. It contains recycled glass from all over the place – workshops, museums, studios, from the 19th century – and, of course, from Ros's secret supply of odds and ends.

The cartoon for the memorial window - 'Joseph's Coat of Many Colours' in Park Row Synagogue, Bristol.

Right: detail of window at St Augustine's church, Scaynes Hill, West Sussex.

Making stained glass windows

A thousand-year-old tradition

and Glossary

Little so-called 'stained glass' is actually glass that has been stained. The pieces of glass are generally coloured throughout their mass; certainly in medieval times this was the case, although by the 16th century colour was also added by applying enamel paints to the surface of clear or coloured glass and then heating the painted piece in a furnace to 'fix' it. **'Staining'** of glass derives from a process that was discovered in the 14th century, whereby existing clear or coloured glass had a chemical (silver nitrate) applied to the surface. This was then heated in a furnace, imparting a stain that penetrated the surface layers of the glass to give a yellow or yellowy-orange colouration. Staining blue glass would therefore give areas of green where the nitrate has been applied.

This seven hundred year old process of 'staining glass' is still in use today – in fact the general principles by which stained and coloured glass windows are made, and the purpose they ultimately serve, have changed little in 1000 years. Entering Ros and Patrick's studio is, in some respects, like going back to the Middle Ages. Apart from the CD player, electric light and spiral staircase much of what one sees would have been seen in the lean-to dwellings that the medieval glaziers occupied against the cathedral walls when

it was a building site: the benches, racks of coloured glass, pieces of lead, hammers, badger brushes, and bottles of wine – for mixing paint (!). Japanese oil-cutters are now pushing out diamond cutters, that in turn replaced red-hot iron and spit; and an electric kiln takes over from the wooden furnaces........

The tradition of the art of stained glass, as established during its heyday in the twelfth to sixteenth centuries, has defined an art form that generally requires different colours to be carried by different pieces of glass. This was very largely due to the technical limitations at that time, when suitable adhesives for gluing pieces of glass together did not exist, and there were very limited techniques of mixing colours within the glass itself. Certain dual-colour effects were possible as we shall later see, but the 'classical' stained glass window comprises pieces of coloured and clear glass being cut to shape and held together by being slotted into strips of lead with an "H" cross-section (**'calms'**) to form panels. Details that shape, colour and form alone have not defined – such as

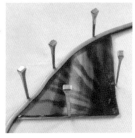

faces, hands, feet, clothing, background scenery etc. - are usually painted onto the surface of some of the pieces of glass once they have been cut to shape. However, in some designs it is possible to dispense with this surface painting altogether: there is only one minute piece of painting in the

Creation Window at Chester, where the initials of many of the people who helped Ros are recorded on a diamond-shaped piece of glass (a **'quarry'**).

Glass Making

The 'secret' of making medieval coloured glass was very largely lost after the mid-16th century when stained glass for various reasons went out of fashion, mainly due to the ideologies of the Reformation and Counter Reformation. So the techniques of making this beautiful glass were almost lost. A few manufacturers kept some aspects of the process going through the seventeenth and eighteenth centuries, but this was a crude product compared with what had gone before. Enamel painting onto the surface of thin clear glass then became the fashion, but when the Gothic Revival got underway in the mid 19th century, this kind of coloured glass was not only unsuitable for 'Neo-Gothic' architecture but stimulated purists to find how the original medieval product was made.

A barrister, Charles Winston, in conjunction with a Midlands glass firm, James Powell, managed to find time between briefs to initiate experiments with glass-making techniques. In 1849 he re-discovered the role played by metal oxides in colouring glass throughout its thickness. Some of the first examples of the new product were used by the Bristol firm, Joseph Bell – where it will be remembered that Ros and Patrick learned much of

their trade – to repair the 14th century window in Bristol cathedral's Lady Chapel. This also gave birth to some really fine 'Victorian' stained glass windows, but within a few years the techniques were married to mass-production processes and the hundreds of thousands of windows that still adorn many of our churches are often un-inspired and repetitive. Nevertheless, the glass itself did share fundamental qualities with that of the Middle Ages, but perhaps lacked its 'mystery', possibly because 'quality control' ensured that the flaws and impurities that gave the ancient product so much of its subtle charm were generally eliminated!

As in medieval times the production of actual coloured glass today is a specialist industry and not part of the stained glass studio's activity, so if Ros had been living and working in medieval times she would have had her sources of suppliers, some of whom might well have been itinerant tinkers, each one holding the 'secret' as to where to obtain particular colours.

Glass is made by fusing sand with wood ash at a very high temperature to give a slightly coloured transparent product, the pale colouration depending upon naturally occurring trace chemicals in the sand and ash. By deliberately adding small amounts of powdered metal oxides into the fused mixture and controlling the amount of air inside the furnace, as well as the rate of cooling, a whole range of colours can be obtained. Glass produced in this way was called **'pot-metal'** glass.

Glass sheets were made in a number of ways, but the most common method after the 12th century was to 'blow it', a process that is still in wide use today – as Ros's visit to Hartley Woods in Sunderland testifies. Invented by the Syrians over 2000 years ago, blowing glass involves taking the molten mass (the **'gather'**) from the crucible by 'gathering' the viscous glob onto the end of an iron

pipe. The glassmaker then blows down the other end so that the mass expands like a balloon. By alternately revolving the pipe, blowing, swinging the balloon to and fro, the 'balloon' grows into a long cylinder or **'muff'**. At a crucial moment before the glass has cooled too much and become rigid, the pipe is cut off and the cylinder cut down its length. Then by a process of alternately re-heating and careful flattening down of the sides of the cylinder a sheet is gradually formed and allowed to cool on a flat surface in the annealing chamber, trying to avoid the glass cracking or crystallising. This is how so-called **'Antique'** glass is made today and still maintains some of the character of medieval glass thanks to the trapped bubbles, striations and uneven thickness.

The various metal oxides involved include manganese for pink and flesh tones, copper or cobalt for blue, and copper again (or iron) for green. Today, other oxides are used to produce more exotic colours, such as antimony for semi-opaque white. Producing red glass (**'ruby'**) has always been something of a problem since the red-producing oxide nearly always made the glass so dark that it was virtually opaque. The solution was to take clear glass and add a thin layer of 'ruby' onto its surface. This process, still used today, known as **'flashing'** is done at the beginning of the 'blowing' of the glass by dipping the pipe with its mass of clear glass into an adjacent crucible of red glass, so that when the balloon is inflated the ruby spreads over the outer surface and to which it adheres as a thin layer. To get deeper shades of red the 'gather' can be repeatedly dipped into the red melt before blowing until the desired density of

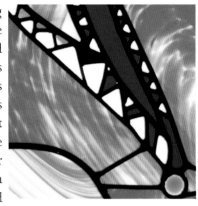

red is achieved – anything up to a dozen times in rare cases. Sometimes the red appears uneven in its density of colour, but this so-called **'streaky'** glass can be used to great effect as can be seen in the Leviathan in the Chester Creation Window. An advantage of red produced this way is that the red layers can subsequently be chipped off to reveal the clear glass beneath, an effect that was frequently put to use in later medieval glass, to give two colours on the same piece of glass. In the 17th century the old Roman process of using a gold compound to produce red-with-a-hint-of-gold was rediscovered and this can be found today in some suppliers' catalogues.

An alternative method of ancient sheet glass production that is still in use today involves spinning the pipe with its molten mass on the end but not blowing, allowing the centrifugal force to mould the glass into a large disc – often up to five feet in diameter. After cooling, this so-called **'Crown Glass'** is cut into pieces, the centre – the **'Bullion'** - either being discarded or ending up as 'quaint' window panes in the local high street teashop. Ros has used a number of these for the letter 'O' in the Genesis text at the foot of the window.

Yet another method, popular in the late 19th and early 20th centuries, involved blowing the glass into a pre-formed rectangular shaped mould, much like the way a bottle is produced today, except that the mould has straight sides so that a thick square 'bottle' was produced that could be broken to give four pieces of rectangular glass – plus the bottom piece. This was known either as 'Early English' (when produced by the firm E.S. Prior) or as **'Norman Slab'** (when produced by Messrs Chance Brothers.)

Early in the 20th century both Louis Comfort Tiffany in the United States and Jacques Gruber in Nancy, amongst others, took advantage of some exotic new techniques in glass-making. They were

particularly fond of fusing sheets of glass of different colours to each other in their windows – producing **'fused glass'** (left). This should not be confused with the placing of two or more sheets on

top of each other – a process known as **'plating'** (left). Mixing different oxides in different parts of the melt, partial cooling and partial re-mixing meant that differing colours could be produced within the same sheet, often interwoven in streaks – another form of so called 'streaky' glass and popular with Art Nouveau glass objects as well as in windows. Many 20th century innovations in glass making found their way into glass destined for stained glass windows, so that the racks in a stained glass window studio today often contain a fascinating variety of glass: 'Antique', 'streaky', Norman Slab, thick slabs, glass with roughened surfaces, 'cloudy' semi-transparent effects, glass of varying thickness, prisms, round lenses, **'blobbies'** (round or spherical pieces of glass), even off-the-shelf ironmongery bathroom pieces!

Window Making

Once the subject matter has been finalised the imagination of the glaziers can get going. Producing a 'first shot' by painting the envisaged window, usually in water colours, is an essential task so that all the parties involved can have their say and agree on what to expect. However Ros's more ambitious 'first shot' has already been mentioned. The window openings are then

accurately measured and a life-sized **'cartoon'** produced, usually painted onto heavy paper, although in the Chester window, as we have seen, it was made by assembling pieces of collage onto the

backing paper. This defines the layout of the window: the sizes and colours of the individual pieces of glass and the lead lines that will run throughout the window to hold them in place. These cartoons can sometimes be works of art in themselves, and the twelve produced by Rosalind are no exception. In medieval times when paper was non-existent the cartoon was generally created on a large whitewashed table onto which the details were drawn and then the glass cut and assembled on the table.

The cartoon is the blueprint for all subsequent work. From it, tracings known as **'cut lines'** are made that define the precise shape of each individual piece of glass, making an allowance for the thickness of the pieces of lead that separate each piece of glass from its neighbour.

Each piece of glass can now be selected and cut to shape against the template. This can be one of the most creative moments in the art of stained glass making, matching what is needed with what is available out of one's store. Bearing in mind Christopher Whall's good advice, the process can at times work the other way round with a particular piece of glass 'demanding' to be used as it is, possibly with very little cutting, that may involve some re-designing with the neighbouring pieces as a result. Such moments can produce minor miracles!

Cutting the glass to shape is normally done with a diamond glass cutter, but for certain intricate pieces with tight curves the job is still best done the way it has been for over a thousand years using a **'grozing iron'**. This medieval piece of equipment allows the glazier to chip away at the edges of the glass and gradually, with luck, the

desired shape emerges without the piece fracturing and ruining hours of work! However, in the hands of skilful and patient operators some fanciful and exotic shapes can be obtained in this way — see, for example, the coloured lines of traffic in the lower panel of Day 1.

It may well be that no existing piece of glass in the rack or the supplier's catalogue will ever produce what is required and some work has to be done

with what is available. **'Acid etching'** enables the flashed colour — for example a thin coat of red that has been fused onto a clear base — to be selectively removed, or partially removed if required, revealing the base colour. The eagle in Day 1 involved much acid etching.

Once all the pieces of glass have been selected and cut to size, the moment comes with most

windows to paint the details — faces, hands, clothing, background etc. - onto the appropriate pieces of glass. However, as already mentioned, in the Chester Creation window there is only one tiny pane that has been given this treatment. A firing in the kiln to 'fix' the paint to the glass follows such painting.

The window is now ready to be assembled, and this takes place on a benchtop by inserting the pieces of glass into the sides of suitably cut lengths of lead 'calms'. Where the pieces of lead meet they are trimmed and soldered on both sides. The 'mosaic' of lead and glass is thus gradually assembled, working away from a side or corner. Each piece of glass is then held in position with nails or stout pins until the next piece is ready to be applied (see photograph on page 37).

When completed, the panels need to be waterproofed, or **'cemented'**, using a compound made from linseed oil, turpentine and calcium carbonate that is forced with a brush under the lead 'calms', completely sealing the window from the weather. They are finally

fixed to the openings in grooves in the surrounding masonry with a sealant (either mortar or mastic). At intervals that coincide with

breaks in the composition brass (or non-ferrous metal), **'saddle bars'** keep the panels rigid by being tied to the lead 'calms'. At Chester these regular lines can be seen every 18 inches or so.

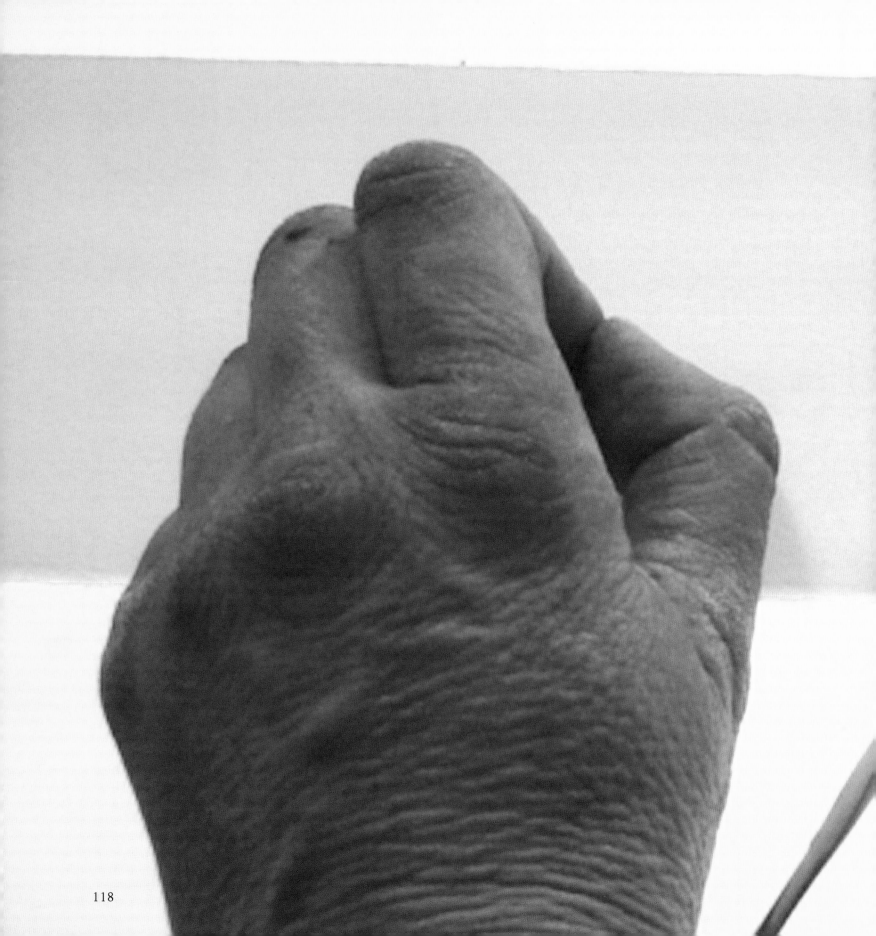

The seventh day

And on the seventh day God ended his work which he had made; and he rested on the seventh day from all his work which he had made. And God blessed the seventh day and sanctified it;
This is the tale of the heavens and the earth when they were created.

Robert Alter translation of Genesis 2:2-4

Painton Cowen

After taking his degree at Cambridge in Geology and spending a year in a steel works in Cardiff, then a year diamond prospecting in Zambia, Painton Cowen worked for some time on the Encyclopaedia Britannica before concentrating on stained glass. He photographed and wrote *Rose Windows* published in 1979 by Thames and Hudson which is still in print: it will be revised and enlarged in a new edition in 2004. From 1979 to 1984 he wrote and did the photography for *A Guide to Stained Glass in Britain* published by Michael Joseph in 1985.

Since then he has worked in computers and is carrying out a study of Dante's Divine Comedy. He shares his time between London and Paris when he is not out photographing rose windows. He and Rosalind Grimshaw have been friends since 1971.

Rosalind Grimshaw

Ros Grimshaw's work follows in the 'Arts and Craft' tradition which seeks to fuse art with industry and everyday life. She started stained glass at Joseph Bell & Son in 1975 until its sad demise in 1996. She now works with her partner, Patrick Costeloe, in their purpose-designed studio in Bristol, carrying on her craft in the tradition of her heroes Edward (Davy) Woore, Wilhemenia Geddes and Harry Clark. Her favourite work is intimate, personal and on a domestic scale but she enjoys the challenge of larger public commissions.

She developed Parkinson's disease in 1984 which has slowed her down but not diminished the quality of her work.

An apology

To my children who have grown up while I was in the studio: Jem, who said I could not work on a large scale; Esther who always noticed when I was going too far; and Francis, who modelled the 'Hand of God'.

The Parkinson's Disease Society

The PDS was established in 1969 and now has 27,000 members and over 288 branches throughout the UK. It provides support, advice and information to people with Parkinson's, their carers, families and friends, and to health and social services professionals involved in management and care. It is a registered charity.

Each year the PDS spends more than £2 million on funding research into the cause, cure and prevention of Parkinson's, and improvements in available treatments. The Society also develops models of good practice in service provision, such as Parkinson's Disease Nurse Specialists and respite care, and campaigns for changes that will improve the lives of people affected by Parkinson's.

215 Vauxhall Bridge Road, London SW1V 1EJ
Tel: 020 7931 8080
Fax: 020 7233 9908
PDS Helpline (free number): 0808 800 0303
(open Monday-Friday, 9.30-5.30)
E-mail: enquiries@parkinsons.org.uk
Website: www.parkinsons.org.uk

There are local PDS branches throughout the UK; please call 020 7932 1306 for details.